SPORTSPEOPLE ON TITANIC

SPORTSPEOPLE ON TITANIC

JAMES W. BANCROFT

FRONTLINE
BOOKS

First published in Great Britain in 2026
by Frontline Books
An imprint of
Pen & Sword Books Ltd
Yorkshire - Philadelphia

ISBN 9781036192075

A CIP catalogue record for this book is available from the British Library

Typeset by Lapiz Digital
Printed and bound in the UK by CPI Group (UK) Ltd,
Croydon, CR0 4YY.

Printed on paper from a sustainable source by
CPI Group (UK) Ltd, Croydon, CR0 4YY

Pen & Sword Books Limited incorporates the imprints of Archaeology, Atlas, Aviation, Battleground, Digital, Discovery, Family History, Fiction, History, Local, Local History, Maritime, Military, Military Classics, Politics, Select, Transport, True Crime, Air World, Claymore Press, Frontline Publishing, Leo Cooper, Remember When, Seaforth Publishing, The Praetorian Press, Wharncliffe Books, Wharncliffe Local History, Wharncliffe Transport, Wharncliffe True Crime and White Owl.

For a complete list of Pen & Sword titles please contact
PEN & SWORD BOOKS LTD
47 Church Street, Barnsley, South Yorkshire, S70 2AS, England
E-mail: enquiries@pen-and-sword.co.uk
Website: www.pen-and-sword.co.uk
or
PEN & SWORD BOOKS
1950 Lawrence Rd, Havertown, PA 19083, USA
E-mail: uspen-and-sword@casematepublishers.com

SPORTSPEOPLE ON TITANIC

JAMES W. BANCROFT

'To social historians [the *Titanic* disaster] is a microcosm of the early 1900s. To nautical enthusiasts it is the ultimate shipwreck. To students of human nature it is an endless fascinating laboratory. For lovers of nostalgia it has the allure of yesterday. For daydreamers it has all those might-have-beens.' – Walter Lord

'We heard several pistol shots, and a great screaming from the decks. The stern lifted high in the air as a tremendous explosion occurred. Then there was another explosion, and the whole forward part of the great steamer went under. The stern at the same time rose still higher, till it was 100 feet in the air like an enormous black figure against the sky. What appeared to be little figures hung for a moment at the rearmost portion of the great black mass, and then dropped into the water. The screaming from the ship was agonising. I never heard such a continued chorus of utter agony.' – Lady Lucy Duff-Gordon

'No panic was evident and I heard no pistol shots. We floated around until dawn, when we saw the lights of the *Carpathia,* and started to row in her direction; as did all the lifeboats. The people aboard the *Carpathia* were fine, and officers, men and passengers cannot be praised too highly. They had made every preparation for our comfort. Quarters and clothes were generously distributed.' – Karl Behr

'The most heartrending part of the whole tragedy was the failure; right after the *Titanic* sank, of those boats which were only partially loaded, to pick up the poor souls in the water. There they were, only four or five hundred yards away, listening to the cries, and still they did not come back. If they had turned back, several hundred more would have been saved. No one can explain it. It was not satisfactorily explained in any investigation. It was just one of the many "Acts of God" running through the whole disaster.' – John Borland Thayer II

'From near at hand and from a distance, too, lifeboats were coming towards us, women occupying rowing seats in many of them, with a man at the tiller. Not a sound escaped their lips; no hysteria was in evidence. Their faces were pinched with cold. The task of raising them from the lifeboats to the ship's deck was difficult. The women with their blistered hands found it hard to climb any ladders. The majority of them were lifted in by a swing which consisted of a board with a rope from each side, connecting with a single large cable.' – Doctor Frank Blackmarr

'Terrible, terrible. No pen can ever depict and no tongue can ever describe adequately the terrors of our experience. Everywhere was a cold, hopeless despair and grief in its most hellish form. Some were dumb with horror; others beat their breasts like things crazed, and a few laughed hysterically and insanely.' – William Carter

In Memoriam

Thomas Andrews
Quiggley Edmond 'Quigg' Baxter
David John 'Dai' Bowen
Thornton Davidson
Charles Alexander Fortune
Mark Fortune
Thomas McCawley
Clarence Moore
Washington Augustus Roebling II
Arthur Larned Ryerson
Peter Sloan
James Clinch Smith
John Borland Thayer II
Charles Duane Williams
Leslie Williams
Frederick Wright

CONTENTS

Introduction xi

RMS *Titanic* 1

Embarkations: 5

- Belfast 5
- Southampton 6
- Cherbourg 13

Making Waves 17

Survivors 25

Lost At Sea 61

Their Hearts Will Go On 69

- *Concise Biographical Tributes* 69
  - Henry 'Harry' Anderson – *Sailing* 69
  - Charles Edward Andrews – *Swimming* 70
  - Thomas Andrews – *Cricket* 72
  - Quiggley Edmond 'Quigg' Baxter – *Athletics / Track and Field, American Football and Ice Hockey* 74
  - Karl Howell Behr – *Lawn Tennis and Ice Hockey* 75
  - David John 'Dai' Bowen – *Boxing* 80
  - William Ernest Carter – *Polo, Racquets and Hunting* 83
  - Lucile Stewart Carter – *Polo, Harness Racing and Swimming* 85
  - Thornton Davidson – *Ice Hockey, Lawn Tennis, Equestrian and Sailing* 86

Sir Cosmo Edmund Duff-Gordon – *Fencing, Martial Arts and Shooting* 88
Francis 'Frank' Dymond – *Boxing* 90
Mark Fortune - *Curling* 93
Charles Alexander Fortune – *Ice Hockey* 94
Frederick Maxfield Hoyt – *Sailing* 95
Joseph Bruce Ismay – *Lawn Tennis, Shooting, Golf, Motoring and Fishing* 96
Thomas McCawley – *Gymnastics, Fencing and Football* 103
Clarence Moore – *Equestrian and Sailing* 105
Major Arthur Godfrey Peuchen – *Sailing* 107
Washington Augustus Roebling II – *Motor Sports and American Football* 109
Arthur Larned Ryerson – *Golf* 111
John Borie 'Jack' Ryerson – *Golf* 112
Peter Sloan – *Association Football and Swimming* 113
James Clinch Smith – *Sailing and Equestrian* 116
Charles Emil Henry Stengel – *Horse Racing* 118
John Borland Thayer II – *Cricket, Baseball and Lacrosse* 121
John Borland 'Jack' Thayer III – *Cricket, Figure Skating, Golf, Racquets and Hunting* 123
Isaac George 'James' Widgery – *Swimming and Bowling* 127
Charles Eugene Williams – *Squash Racquets* 129
Leslie Williams – *Boxing* 131
Charles Duane Williams – *Lawn Tennis* 133
Richard Norris Williams II – *Lawn Tennis* 135
Hugh Woolner – *Rugby Union, Rowing and Athletics / Track and Field* 140
Frederick Wright – *Squash Racquets* 142
Sporting Connections 145
Newspaper Reports and Inquiries 147
Bibliography and Research Sources 171
Index 179

INTRODUCTION

The Titanic disaster remains in the public consciousness because it reminds us that we are vulnerable, no matter how much we might be reassured by those in authority, and that the elements will have their way.

While pushing relentlessly westward through the waves at full steam ahead across the North Atlantic Ocean towards New York on the night of 14/15 April 1912, the brand new 'unsinkable' luxury liner RMS *Titanic* collided with a frozen mass of ice. The crash caused a series of large gashes or punctures dotted along about 300 feet of the starboard front side of the ship; about a third of her total length. She sank in less than three hours, taking about two out of every three of her passengers and crew with her – a terrible loss of life.

Among those on board were no less than thirty-three individuals, American, British and Canadian, who were involved in twenty-seven various sports before and after the disaster, including the Olympic Games, the Wimbledon championships, and several other national championships; or in some cases they played sport for leisure. Half of them lost their lives. They included the managing director of the White Star Line, and one of its foremost designers, who had both been involved in sport in their younger days. This is the story of who they were, what happened to them during the disaster, and what the future held for those who survived.

The night *Titanic* sank, the Cable Ship *Carpathia* was on its way from New York to Gibraltar and was fortunately in the region. On receiving a distress signal from *Titanic,* Captain Arthur Rostron immediately set a heroic course towards the disaster area. After working through dangerous ice fields, *Carpathia* arrived at the scene at 4 am in the morning of 15 April. All the cold and traumatised survivors in the lifeboats had spent the night drifting in the sea about a mile from the disaster site, until *Carpathia* came into sight at dawn and picked them up.

Carpathia arrived back in New York with just over 700 survivors on the evening of 18 April, where they were taken off at Pier 54. Meanwhile, the crew were taken to Pier 61 by a tender named the *George Starr.* There seems to have been an attempt to keep the crew away from awkward questions until they had been briefed.

While on the rescue ship, some of the survivors formed a committee to honour the bravery of Captain Rostron and his crew, which included lawn tennis player Karl Behr and Hugh Woolner, who was a Cambridge blue. When they landed back in New York the committee put out the following statement:

> At 11.40 on the evening of Sunday, April 14, on a cold and starlit night, the *Titanic* struck an iceberg. The look-outs reported the iceberg before the collision, but the vessel was unable to avoid it. Orders were promptly given to put on lifebelts, and the lifeboats were launched and distress signals sent out by wireless and rockets fired.
>
> The vessel sank at 2.20 am, on Monday. The *Carpathia* arrived at 4 am, and took the rescued passengers from the boats. The captain and officers of the *Carpathia* gave the most touching care and attention to all the passengers when they were taken on board.
>
> Every individual on board had been allocated a life-jacket, but the ship carried 14 lifeboats, two smaller boats, and four collapsible boats. The boats were entirely insufficient to enable all those on board to escape.
>
> There was no panic on board while the women and children were leaving the ship in the boats; everyone believed that it was simply a measure of precaution. Several women were torn from their husbands when the orders were given to rescue only the

> women. Even then several refused to leave, and were drowned with their husbands. One woman died in a lifeboat, and three others succumbed after reaching the *Carpathia*.

The RMS *Titanic* disaster is one of history's most catastrophic human tragedies. It harbours many heartbreaking stories about its ill-fated passengers and crew, whose lives were painfully shattered by what they saw and experienced during that one dreadful incident. Most of the people who survived the disaster never really got over it.

James W. Bancroft, 2026

RMS *TITANIC*

The White Star Line was established in 1845. They began the business of shipbrokers in Liverpool, from where they initially leased and chartered ships to operate packet sailing to the east coast of the United States. They started to use the name White Star Line of Boston Packets in 1849 and cut it short to just White Star Line after they started sending ships to Australia. Business increased after the discovery of gold in Australia in 1851, and this enabled them to purchase the vessels they used.

The company's bank failed in 1867 and with massive debts it was forced into bankruptcy. However, in the following year, Thomas Henry Ismay purchased the bankrupt company, with the intention of operating large steamships on the North Atlantic service between Liverpool and New York. During a game of billiards, Ismay was approached by Gustav Wolff and his uncle, who offered to finance the new Line. A partnership with Harland and Wolff was established in the summer of 1869, the agreement being that Harland and Wolff would build ships exclusively for the White Star Line. On the death of Thomas Ismay in 1899, he was succeeded as the chairman and managing director of the White Star Line by his son, J. Bruce Ismay. In 1907 Bruce met Lord William Pirrie of Harland and Wolff, to discuss White Star Line's answer to Cunard Line's recently unveiled *Lusitania* and *Mauretania* vessels. Their idea was to build three 'Olympic' class ships at Harland and Wolff that were intended to be marvels of engineering.

The Royal Mail Ship *Titanic* was a Liverpool-registered ocean liner built for the trans-Atlantic passenger and mail service between Southampton and New York. She was constructed at the Harland and Wolff shipyard in Belfast and was launched on 31 May 1911. *Titanic* weighed over 46,000 tonnes and was valued at £1.5 million. She included sixteen watertight doors that could be closed automatically from the bridge, sealing off the compartments if necessary; the ship would still stay afloat even if four of the compartments were to flood– or would it? This system prompted White Star to describe the vessel as practically unsinkable.

Titanic was the second of the 'Olympic' class of luxury liners to be built, her slightly smaller sister ship, RMS *Olympic,* having sailed on her maiden voyage on 14 June 1911. During her fifth voyage on 20 September 1911, *Olympic,* with Captain Edward Smith on board, had a serious collision with the British cruiser HMS *Hawke.* Because of the accident, *Titanic* was moved out of dry-dock on 6 March 1912 to allow for *Olympic* to have a propeller blade fixed, which had become damaged during the collision. Consequently, *Titanic* was not completed until 2 April and was fatefully re-scheduled to begin her maiden voyage on Wednesday, 10 April 1912.

A third ship in the 'Olympic' class, RMS *Britannic,* was launched just before the start of the First World War, on 26 February 1914. She was later requisitioned as a hospital ship sailing between the United Kingdom and the Dardanelles, where she hit an enemy naval mine and sank on 21 November 1916.

Titanic was built to accommodate about 3,000 passengers and over 900 crew members, and being a Royal Mail ship, she was carrying about as many sacks of mail as people. *Titanic* had four funnels, although only three of them released steam from the boilers and the one at the rear served no purpose other than the fact that the designers thought the ship would look more impressive with four funnels rather than just three.

The ship was designed to provide the ultimate in luxury travel. There was a swimming pool with an adjacent Turkish bath suite, a state-of-the-art gymnasium, an à la carte restaurant, and the Café Parisian. However, the ship's main feature was the Grand Staircase. Built from solid English oak, and enhanced with wrought iron, the decorated glass domes above were designed to let in as much natural light as possible. To have sailed on 'The voyage of the century' aboard RMS *Titanic*, the world's largest and most luxurious vessel afloat at that time, was like being one of the first people to fly on *Concorde*. It was described at the time as 'a floating palace' – a combination of Mayfair and Bel Air on water!

Despite the luxury, one of the decisions that eventually brought Bruce Ismay notoriety was to go against the advice of the Board of Trade, and to reduce the number of lifeboats from forty-eight to sixteen, with four collapsible rafts to bring the total number of lifeboats to twenty. The company never envisaged that the passengers and crew would have to be evacuated all at once, and instead the lifeboats were intended to be used to transfer passengers off the stricken ship to a nearby vessel that had hopefully arrived to offer assistance. The view of the time was that 'every ship should be her own lifeboat'.

The various types of lifeboats on board were all stored in six separate areas of the top deck. Looking towards the front of the ship, regular lifeboat numbers 7, 5, 3 and emergency 1 were at the front, starboard (right-hand) side, with numbers 4, 6, 8 and emergency 2 at the portside (left-hand) side. The two smaller wooden cutters, apparently known as the captain's emergency boats, were already hanging in their crane-like devices (davits) for incidents such as someone falling overboard and struggling in the sea. Lifeboat numbers 9, 11, 13 and 15 were situated at the rear starboard side of the ship, with numbers 10, 12, 14 and 16 at the rear portside. There were four dinghies with collapsible canvas sides, lettered A, B, C and D.

It was considered that the fourteen wooden lifeboats were capable of carrying sixty-five people in each, for a total of 896; with forty people in each of the two emergency lifeboats, for a total of eighty, and forty-seven in each of the four collapsible dinghies, for a total of 188; making a grand total of 1,164 people; which was dreadfully insufficient for the more than 2,200 passengers on board. It is difficult to comprehend, but at the time of the disaster, lifeboat accommodation was regulated according to the tonnage of the ship and not the number of passengers and crew. With these figures in mind, it would seem that in practice, the lifeboats were not seaworthy if they had more than forty passengers in them. Adding to the problem was the fact that the crew had not been sufficiently trained in the use of the davits – the lifeboat launching equipment.

At the time of the launch of RMS *Titanic,* the *Daily Telegraph* published some particulars about the ship, which, together with her sister ship RMS *Olympic,* had cost £3 million:

> Tons, 45,000; length between perpendiculars, 882 feet; breadth, 92 feet 6 inches; depth 62 feet; speed, 21 knots; built 1911. The largest beam in the *Titanic* weighs more than 4 tons, and measures 92 feet. The longest steel plates are 36 feet, and there are two and a half million rivets in the ship. The *Titanic* will have, in addition to dining saloons, lounges, drawing rooms and smoking rooms, several restaurants and veranda cafe. She is to have a splendidly equipped Turkish bath, a swimming bath, and a full-sized racquets court. Passenger accommodation is planned for 750 first-class, 515 second-class, and 1,100 third-class, and the crew will number 860.

Titanic arrived at Southampton during the first hour of 4 April 1912, and by midday men were turning up at the dock to sign on as members of the crew. The ship made a majestic sight as she was moored for five days in berth 43 at Dock Gate 4, the entrance to the Eastern Dock in Southampton. People from all walks of life began embarking on her on 10 April 1912, for what was to be the trip of a lifetime. Many were looking forward to starting new lives in North America.

EMBARKATIONS

The crew and passengers embarked on the ship at various ports; some at Belfast, some at Southampton and some at Cherbourg. Some passengers also embarked at Queenstown (now Cobh) in southern Ireland, but none of these are relevant to this publication and so are not included here.

Belfast

The chief designer of *Titanic* was an Irishman named Thomas Andrews, known as 'Tommie', who made a point of sailing with a team of mechanics on the maiden voyages of many of his ships; and *Titanic* would be no different. They were known as the Guarantee Group, and Tommie boarded in his home city of Belfast and took a cabin on A Deck. He left his wife and daughter behind to embark for the liner's initial trip to Southampton. Tommie was a keen cricketer, and all the men in his family played the sport.

Some members of the crew also embarked at Belfast on 25 March 1912, and as they travelled with the ship, they were tasked to get it prepared for the journey across the Atlantic Ocean. Among them was Peter Sloan, a married man from Liverpool, who journeyed to Belfast to be taken on, having just been promoted to chief electrician, for which he would receive wages of £6 a month. He enjoyed football and swimming, and won several trophies for the latter. He had also been involved in two previous shipping accidents. It seems that he had planned to meet another woman when *Titanic* arrived in New York.

Thomas McCawley embarked at Belfast as a permanent physical instructor in the gymnasium. He was a former collier, who had served with the Manchester Regiment during the Anglo-Boer War of 1899-1902. During his military service he was awarded first-class certificates in gymnastics and fencing. There were good sport facilities on *Titanic,* which were exclusive to first-class passengers, and the gymnasium was segregated by gender and age. It was situated near the forward grand staircase, along the starboard side of the top deck. It was a brightly-lit room equipped with state-of-the-art apparatus, including two electric camels, an electric horse, a rowing machine, a punching bag, a weightlifting machine and mechanical bicycles, and McCawley assisted the passengers in using the devices.

Southampton

In his 1936 book *Titanic and Other Ships,* Officer Charles Lightoller recorded:

> Unfortunately whilst in Southampton we had a re-shuffle amongst the senior officers, owing to the *Olympic* being laid up, the ruling lights of the White Star Line thought it would be a good plan to send the chief officer of the *Olympic,* just for one voyage, as chief officer of the *Titanic,* to help, with his experience of her sister ship. This doubtful policy threw both Murdoch and me out of our stride; and apart from the disappointment of having to step back in our rank, caused quite a little confusion. Murdoch from chief, took over my duties as First, I stepped back on Blair's toes, as Second, and picked up the many threads of his job, whilst he – luckily for him as it turned out – was left behind. The other officers remained the same. However, a couple of days in Southampton saw each of us settled in our new positions and familiar with our duties.

Officer Blair left the ship on 9 April, and as it was due to sail on the following day, he would have been rushing about getting ready to disembark. In his rush he forgot to hand over the key to the locker containing the binoculars for the look-outs in the crow's nest. It was to be hoped they would not get into any difficulty which would require them.

Northamptonshire-born Frederick Wright, and a Bristolian named Isaac George Widgery, known as James, embarked at Southampton, as the instructor in the squash racquets court and the swimming baths attendant respectively.

During *Olympic* and *Titanic's* design stages, Bruce Ismay requested that a squash court be installed on the vessels, the first time that such an amenity had been incorporated into a ship's design. It is entirely possible that the inclusion of this key feature may have been a direct result of his brief time at Harrow School.

In a letter to his sister, Wright described the ship as 'the best' - implying it was better than the *Olympic* liner on which he had previously worked.

The squash court was situated at the bow of G Deck and measured 30 feet long by 20 feet wide. There was a spectator's gallery on F Deck overlooking the court. It could be entered only by a separate flight of stairs starting on D Deck, from where a passenger could descend the three decks past the viewing platform to G Deck.

To play squash passengers could purchase tickets from *Titanic*'s enquiry office on C Deck, which would have cost them 2 shillings (about 10 pence today) or 50 cents for the use of the court for half an hour, which included the services of the professional player if desired. Passengers were permitted to use the court for up to an hour at a time, unless there were no other passengers wanting to play. Those wishing to play could purchase balls and hire or purchase rackets on board from the professional player managing the court.

There was a heated swimming pool on the forward section of F Deck, which measured 30 feet by 14 feet, although it was comparatively small and was usually referred to as a 'Baths'. It was 5 feet 4 inches deep at one end, and 4 feet 6 inches at the other. Heated salt water from a tank and cold sea water were pumped into the pool as soon as the ship was out at sea. The room offered thirteen changing cubicles and two shower stalls. It cost 1 shilling or 50 cents to use, but was open to men free of charge for two hours' early morning exercise. For his role as an attendant at the swimming baths, James Widgery received monthly wages of £3 15s.

Liverpool-born Bruce Ismay sometimes travelled with his ships on their maiden voyages, and he boarded *Titanic* at Southampton with his secretary and valet, occupying room B-102. He had been a talented tennis player in his younger days, having won the Waterloo Championships in Liverpool, and the Northern Mixed Doubles Championships at Manchester in 1883, which was later moved to the All England Club at Wimbledon; technically making him a Wimbledon champion.

Another Liverpudlian crew member was Charles Andrews, who signed-on as a saloon steward. He was a keen swimmer, for which he is reported to have gained several awards.

Frank Dymond signed-on as a fireman. He was a West Country man, who was a keen boxer. He served in the Royal Navy and afterwards joined the White Star Line. His family considered him to have been a 'hard man', who would take part in boxing bouts on the ships on which he was serving.

David 'Dai' Bowen was from the town of Treherbert, and Leslie Williams was from Tonypandy, both in south Wales. They were considered to be highly promising boxers, and their names appear on the passenger lists as 'pugilists'. They were on their way to the United States for a series of boxing contests. In a letter to his mother Dai Bowen wrote, 'This is a lovely boat, she is very near as big as Treherbert.'

William Carter of Philadelphia and his wife Lucile had booked to travel on RMS *Olympic,* which departed from Southampton on 3 April 1912, but they changed their minds and arrived at Southampton to board *Titanic* with quite an entourage. They had with them their two children, Lucile Polk, who had been at boarding school in England, and William 'Billy' Thornton, along with Lucile's maid, William's manservant, and their chauffeur. They occupied first-class cabins B-96 and B-98. They also brought on board some polo ponies, two dogs, and their 1912 Renault type CB Coupe de Ville motor car.

Willie, as he was known, was a good horseman and a keen polo player, and the family had been staying at Rotherby Manor near Melton Mowbray in Leicestershire, where he had played a few games of polo, and had also found time to go hunting with the local foxhounds.

Baltimore socialite Lucile was known to be athletic and quite daring, and was reportedly the first woman to play polo riding astride the horse instead of side-saddle. It was also said she drove a coach-and-four through a main street in her home city.

It was originally thought that the Thayer party boarded at Cherbourg, but it is recorded that Jack Thayer was on *Titanic*'s deck at Southampton when she nearly collided with another ship in the harbour (the *New York*), so he must have boarded at Southampton instead. He gave a description of what he saw to his father, and recorded that an old man said the collision was a bad omen. In addition, Marian Thayer sent a telegram to her sister on 10 April mentioning the *New York* incident, and that her husband had had the presence of mind to take five photographs of it.

John Borland Thayer II was a director and second vice-president of the Pennsylvania Railroad Company, and a prominent sportsman in his younger days, especially at baseball, lacrosse and cricket, which was a sport that rivalled baseball in Pennsylvania at the time. John had been in Berlin as guest of the American consul general. Having left three of his children in America, he was travelling with his socialite wife Marian, his 17-year-old son, Jack, and their 42-year-old Pennsylvanian maid Margaret Fleming. Jack was also a keen cricketer, and in later life he became involved in several sports in Pennsylvania. John and Marian occupied cabin C-68 and Jack was nearby in C-70 on the port side of C Deck.

First-class passenger Clarence Moore was known as one of the finest horsemen in Washington DC. He was also a good sailor, being a member of the Chevy Chase Equestrian Club and the New York Yacht Club. He had been in England to acquire good quality foxhounds for the Loudon Hunt in Virginia, of which he was hunt master. He purchased fifty pairs in the north of England, although they did not return with him on *Titanic.* He also travelled up to Liverpool to watch the Grand National, in which Bloodstone, belonging to Bruce Ismay's brother, came second.

Mark and Mary Fortune had been on vacation in Europe with their three daughters, Ethel Flora, Alice Elizabeth and Mabel Helen, and a son named Charles Alexander, who was the youngest of the four children. While in Cairo earlier in the year, their 24-year-old daughter Alice had been approached by a fortune teller, who warned, 'You are in danger every time you travel on the sea, for I see you adrift in an open boat. You will lose everything but your life.' She had gained an admirer in 28-year-old William Thomson Sloper, 'because she was a pretty girl and am excellent dancing partner.' He had cancelled his trip on another ship to travel on *Titanic.* However, Alice was engaged to someone back home in Winnipeg. The Fortune family boarded as first-class passengers and occupied cabins C-23-25-27. Mark was a keen curler, and 19-year-old Charles had graduated from Bishop's College in Lennoxville, Quebec, with citations for academic and athletic excellence, mainly in the sport of ice hockey.

Two New Yorkers named Frederick and Jane Ann Hoyt boarded at Southampton as first-class passengers in cabin C-93. Frederick was a noted member of the Larchmont Yacht Club and the New York Yacht Club. He owned several prestigious yachts and took part in international races.

Harry Anderson, a stockbroker on Wall Street in New York, was also a member of the Larchmont Yacht Club, and the New York Yacht Club. It was stated that he had been in London for business and pleasure, and he occupied first-class cabin E-12. His wife had stayed at home in New York, but he had a Chow Chow dog with him.

Major Arthur Peuchen was an officer in the Queen's Own Rifles of Canada, who had acted as marshalling officer at the coronation of King George V and Queen Mary in 1911. He was a keen yachtsman, and as rear-commodore of the Royal Canadian Yacht Club, he owned a 65-foot yacht named *Vreda*, which had crossed the Atlantic on its own steam. His mother had recently passed away in Toronto.

Major Peuchen was a highly successful businessman, in his capacity as the president of Standard Chemical, Iron and Lumber Company of Canada Limited, which manufactured chemicals to make explosives. They had a refinery in London during the pre-First World War arms race between Britain and Germany, so he had paid a visit to the War Office. He sent a telegram to his wife back in Toronto, stating 'Sailing on Titanic – Arthur.' He boarded at Southampton as a first-class passenger in cabin C-104, for what would be his fortieth transatlantic voyage.

Washington Roebling II had been involved with his cousin in the construction of the Brooklyn Bridge in New York, before becoming a pioneer of the early days of motor sport. He was returning from a long road trip in Europe with his chauffeur Frank Stanley in a Mercer Fiat motor car. He was accompanied by his friend and fellow native of Trenton, Stephen Blackwell, who was on an extended holiday because of health reasons. They were first-class passengers in cabin A-24.

Charles Williams was a married man and a successful racquets player. He had won the English Open title in 1911, and the World Championship early in 1912. He described himself as a 'sportsman' on the passenger list, and was on his way to defend his title in New York. Fortunately, his wife and new-born son remained at home in Harrow.

Hugh Woolner was educated at Trinity College in Cambridge, where, being a tall and hefty man, he gained a blue for throwing the hammer against Oxford. He was also a keen rugby union player and rower. He was a London stockbroker and travelled in cabin C-52. The son of a celebrated sculptor, his mother had passed away a few weeks before he sailed.

Also boarding at Southampton were Richard and Sallie Beckwith and Sallie's 19-year-old daughter from her first marriage, Helen Monypenny Newsom. Helen had been courting the brother of a friend of hers, a New York tennis player named Karl Behr, but it seems Mrs Newman had particular plans for her daughter's future and had taken her on a 'grand trip' to Europe to try to discourage the relationship by keeping them apart. They would get a surprise when they got to Cherbourg, because Mr Behr was waiting to board there. They occupied cabins 35 and 47 on the starboard side of D Deck, above where the actual blow was struck.

After leaving Southampton, there was a major problem below decks, unknown to the passengers above. Leading Fireman Fred Barrett reported: 'Just after departure from Southampton I and about ten other men received orders to empty the coal bunker in boiler room six, where a fire had been discovered.'

It took them three days to get the fire under control, although they could not extinguish it completely, and when Fred went back to see the extent of the damage he noted that the bulkhead was damaged from top to bottom, the lower half being warped at the back and the upper half being warped at the front.

Fireman John Dilley stated: 'From the day we sailed the *Titanic* was on fire, in bunker 6, and my sole duty, together with eleven other men, had been to fight that fire. We had made no headway against it.'

Titanic's departure on 10 April 1912 was almost marred by another disaster. As mentioned briefly earlier, when leaving her dock soon after noon, she was pulled out into Southampton Water by three tugs. As the vast ship moved along the quay, she passed the liner *Oceanic*, with a distance of about 50 yards separating the vessels, until she came opposite the liner *New York*. The seven ropes holding the *New York* to the quay began to strain, and she was being drawn towards *Titanic* by suction. Suddenly, some of the ropes snapped and the stern of the vessel began to veer round towards *Titanic*. The great ship came to a standstill, and as soon as the rope had been disconnected the three tugs went to the assistance of the *New York*. At this time barely 15 feet separated the two vessels. Fortunately, the tugs were able to secure the *New York* and get her back to the quay. *Titanic* backed up about 200 yards, and eventually the three tugs were connected to her again. Another start was made, and this time the other ships were passed without mishap.

Cherbourg

Thomas Andrews wrote a note from Cherbourg to his wife: 'We reached here in nice time and took on board quite a number of passengers. The two little tenders looked well; you will remember we built them about a year ago. We expect to arrive at Queenstown about 10:30 am tomorrow. The weather is fine and everything shaping for a good voyage. I have a seat at the doctor's table.'

The harbour at Cherbourg-Octeville was the second-largest artificial harbour in the world at that time, and *Titanic* sailed into it at early evening on 10 April. An hour and a half later, two tenders named *Nomadic* and *Traffic* had brought 281 passengers to the ship to be embarked.

Among the single men who boarded at Cherbourg was Karl Behr, who had followed a career in banking, and in that capacity had organised a business trip to Europe to follow Helen Newsom (see above). He was a member of the United States Davis Cup team in 1907 and in the same year had reached the fourth round of the singles at Wimbledon, finishing as a runner-up in the doubles. He was in stateroom C-148.

Canadians Thornton and Orian Davidson had been invited by Orian's parents, Charles and Clara Hays, to accompany them on a business trip to London, but the couple had left the party in England for a trip to the continent. However, Mr and Mrs Hays received news that their older daughter was having trouble with her pregnancy, so they boarded *Titanic* at Southampton, with their maid, Mary Anne Perrault, and a friend of the family named Vivian Ponsonby Payne. Thornton and Orian joined the ship at Cherbourg and took cabin B-71. Thornton came from a well-known sporting family and excelled at several sports. He was an accomplished sailor, a successful ice hockey player, a good horseman, and a fine lawn tennis player.

Another Canadian first-class passenger who joined the ship at Cherbourg was Quigg Baxter, the son of a wealthy diamond merchant and banker. He excelled at athletics / track and field, American football and ice hockey, until an ice hockey accident had left him blind in one eye. He had been coaching ice hockey in Switzerland and France, and had been joined by his mother, Helene, and his sister Mary, who was known as 'Zette'. He had met a cabaret singer named Bertha Mayne while in Brussels and the two had become a couple. He was determined to take Bertha back to Canada with him, so he acquired cabin C-90 for her in the name of Mme DeVilliers, which was her stage name. He put his mother and sister in cabin B-60, while he took cabin B-58, which had an access door between them.

Sir Cosmo and Lady Lucy Duff-Gordon, along with her secretary, Laura Francatelli, boarded at Cherbourg, for some reason under the names Mr and Mrs Morgan. Lucy had fashion salons in London, Chicago and New York, and they were going to America because there was a problem with the lease on one of them. They paid nearly £40 for their tickets, and Sir Cosmo occupied cabin A-16, while Lucy took cabin A-20. Sir Cosmo was a keen sportsman and was a member of the International Olympic Committee, having gained an Olympic fencing silver medal at what was known as the Interim Games held in Athens in 1906. He was also a wrestler and took part in the mixed martial art known as Bartitsu, a form of judo, and even took part in pistol-duelling events.

Arthur and Emily Ryerson had received the devastating news that their son, Arthur Junior, had been killed in a car crash back in Philadelphia, so they were desperate to get back home. As the owner of the Otsego Golf Club, Arthur Senior was one of two western delegates who went to New York in 1894 to assist in the formation of the United States Golf Association. They were accompanied on the voyage by two of their daughters, Emily and Susan, known as 'Suzette', and their son John Borie, who, at the age of 13, was already showing great promise on the golf course. A maid and governess were also with them, and they occupied cabins B-57-63 and B-66.

James Clinch Smith was a member of most of New York's elite clubs. He was a skilful yachtsman and a multi-prize-winning rider at the New York Horse Show. He had built his own track in his hometown of Smithtown in New York, which had been named after one of his ancestors. He had been in Paris to visit his wife, who had organised an all-women cabaret band, and occupied cabin A-7.

Charles and Annie Stengel were returning from a trip to Europe. Charles was a New Jersey leather manufacturer who was described in newspapers as 'A prominent New York racehorse owner'. They travelled in first-class cabin C-116, which was close to the engines.

Charles Duane Williams and his son Richard Norris, often known as R. Norris Williams, had travelled from their home in Geneva to Cherbourg, on their way to visit Richard's mother in America. Duane is credited with helping to establish the International Tennis Federation and for promoting the sport in Switzerland. Having become the Swiss lawn tennis champion in 1911, Norris was on his way to play some tournaments in the United States and to enrol at Harvard University.

When embarkation at Cherbourg was completed, *Titanic* set sail for Queenstown, in southern Ireland. She dropped anchor at Roches Point outer anchorage and the officers welcomed aboard 123 more passengers, before the grand ship got out into the open sea on its voyage westward to New York.

MAKING WAVES

For all her opulence and unsinkable reputation, many members of *Titanic*'s passengers and crew expressed uneasy forebodings about the ship (see *Titanic Disaster: Omens, Mysteries and Misfortunes of the Doomed Liner*, 2023). One of these was Esther Hart, who was travelling to Winnipeg, Canada, with her husband, Benjamin, and their 7-year-old daughter Eva. Esther was already concerned that they were leaving her father and mother behind who were quite old and not in the best of health. She had never had any kind of premonitions before, but she considered all the talk of the ship being unsinkable was flying in the face of God, stating: 'I can honestly say that from the moment the journey to Canada was mentioned till the time we got aboard *Titanic,* I never contemplated with any other feelings but those of dread and uneasiness.'

Her forebodings caused her to be particularly wary of how the ship was performing, and she was unconvinced when told the ship was so big that it was not supposed to roll badly as it pounded through the waves. She slept during the day and stayed awake at night, seemingly presuming if there was going to be a problem it would happen during the hours of darkness. She wrote:

> Anyhow it rolls enough for me, I shall never forget it. It is nice weather but awfully windy and cold. They say we may get into New York Tuesday night but we were really due early on Wednesday morning. The sailors say we have had a wonderful passage, up to now there has been no tempest, but God knows what it must be like when there is one. This rough expanse of water, no land in sight and the ship rolling from side to side is very wonderful, though they say this ship does not roll on account of its size. We have met some nice

> people on board and so it has been nice so far. But oh, the long, long days and nights it's the longest week I ever spent in my life.

Mr Andrews spent most of his voyage on *Titanic* making notes on how the ship could be improved. He was very popular with the crew, and during the voyage Chief Baker Charles Joughin prepared a special loaf of bread for him. He usually dined on the next table to a twice-married New Yorker named Eleanor Cassebeer, and she later stated he had mentioned to her that, 'the vessel was started on her maiden voyage before she was finished'. However, he also stated that the ship was 'as nearly perfect as human brains can make her'.

Steward Henry Etches was in charge of eight first-class portside cabins on B Deck, including that of Thomas Andrews in A-36. Etches reported at the cabin of Mr Andrews every morning at 7 am, describing how he used to be busy all the time working on his new ship. Apparently, Mr Andrews had charts rolled up by the side of his bed, as well as papers of all description on his desk, and he was constantly taking notes on any improvements that could be made. Etches would see him at other points during the days aboard, mainly on E Deck, and always with an entourage, taking notes for improvements.

On Friday, 12 April, as Mr Andrews was going in for dinner he was met by a fellow Belfast native in Nurse Stewardess Mary Sloan, and they started to chat. They talked of home, and how Mr Andrews' father and his wife were unwell. The nurse congratulated him on the beauty and perfection of the ship, to which he responded that the only part he did not like about *Titanic* was that it was taking them further away from home with every hour. His usual dinner companion, Dr William O'Loughlin, called to him hurry up or they might be late, but Mr Andrews was reluctant to go. Nurse Sloan noticed that he had, 'a very sad expression'.

During the voyage seven individuals on board had formed what they referred to as 'Our Coterie'. This was based on a famous fashionable set of English aristocrats and intellectuals of the

Edwardian period, known as 'The Coterie'. James Clinch Smith and Hugh Woolner were members of this seemingly exclusive club.

Saloon Steward Tom Whiteley remembered:

> Orders had been issued Sunday to make the dinner the finest ever served on a ship, regardless of expense, and the orders were carried out. The one topic of conversation was the new boat and the speed she was making... At one time Doctor O'Loughlin stood up, and, raising a glass of champagne, cried, 'Let us drink to the mighty *Titanic.*' With cries of approval, everybody drank to the toast. I believe it was generally thought by all of those at the tables that the *Titanic* would reach New York late Tuesday or early Wednesday morning, and the captain and other officers were planning a big banquet after the landing in anticipation of the trip record breaker. The dinner broke up shortly before 9 o'clock, and the men retired to the smoking rooms, while some of the women went to their staterooms, and others strolled along the promenade.

Because of the location of their cabin, Charles and Annie Stengel became aware that the ship was going faster every day. On 13 April, Mr Stengel placed a wager with some other first-class passengers as to who could estimate the closest to the headway the liner was making. It was calculated that the ship made 546 knots. Mr Stengel would need to be careful when it came to his betting as there were three men with notorious reputations for being tricksters and card sharps among the first-class passengers. One of these was George Brereton, known as George Brayton on *Titanic*. He was an American gambler and fraudster, who embarked at Southampton as a first-class passenger. He was known to have been in the first-class smoking room stalking a victim when the collision occurred. He was rescued in lifeboat 9.

During the voyage, passenger Adolphe Saalfeld referred to his, '... approval of a luncheon featuring soup, fillet of plaice, a loin chop with cauliflower and fried potatoes. The weather is calm and fine, the sky overcast. After a fair night's rest and an excellent breakfast I am enjoying a promenade in glorious weather. The wind is fresh and the sea moderate, but on this big boat one hardly notices any movement.'

Many passengers took regular strolls along the promenades after dinner, and as they did so, it is interesting to speculate whether some of them became aware that there did not seem to be enough lifeboats for the vast number of people on board the ship and whether they expressed concern at what would happen if there was a reason to have to evacuate. But they were no doubt consoled by the fact that they were on board the 'unsinkable' *Titanic*.

On Saturday, 13 April, Elizabeth and Mary Lines of New York finished lunch in the first-class dining room on D Deck, and continued their habit of stopping for coffee in the adjoining reception room afterwards. Captain Smith and Bruce Ismay, whom Mary recognised from living in New York, came and sat at a table close to them, and they began to discuss the possibility of having the last boilers lit. Could this have been because of their desire to make the ship go faster?

Later that day, George and Eleanor Widener were standing on the first-class promenade deck talking to Bruce Ismay, when Captain Smith came walking by as he was making his way towards the back of the ship. Without a word, he passed a telegram to Mr Ismay: an ice warning received from the *Baltic* at 1.42 pm. Ismay put in his pocket and walked away. Marian Thayer and Emily Ryerson also met Mr Ismay on the promenade deck, and he showed them the telegram.

After doing his rounds on 14 April, Mr Andrews was of the opinion that all was shipshape and Bristol fashion: 'Today I made my usual inspection of the ship. I talked to a few people on the deck and then went around the ship to see if there was anyone who could use a little help... No problems of great importance have risen so far. As passengers are starting to get comfortable in the ship there has been less for me to do. So far, it's been a delightful cruise for everyone.'

At about 9 pm Officer Moody told Officer Lightoller that he estimated they should reach the ice region by about 11 pm, and both Lightoller and Captain Smith remarked on how quickly the temperature was dropping, yet the weather was clear and the sea unusually calm. It was a starlit night, which Lightoller believed would reflect light off any icebergs that might be nearby. At 9.20 pm Captain Smith, in reference to some iceberg warnings they had received, left the bridge and gave Officer Lightoller the instructions: 'If in the slightest degree doubtful, let me know.' About ten minutes later, Officer Moody telephoned the crow's nest and told the men there to keep a sharp lookout for small ice and to pass the word to subsequent watches.

In the crow's nest keeping watch were Fred Fleet and Reg Lee. Reg reported later: 'There was a good deal of haze ahead. It thickened, but the speed of the vessel was not slackened.' Just after seven bells (11:30 pm), Fred saw a black mass ahead, immediately struck three straight bells and telephoned the bridge. He reported: 'Iceberg right ahead.' While he was still on the telephone, the ship started veering to the left (portside), and the crow's nest began to shake.

Just before midnight on Sunday, 14 April, RMS *Titanic* began to send out signals of distress stating: 'We have struck an iceberg.'

Earlier in the day, the Marconi wireless operators Jack Phillips and Harold Bride had received messages from other ships concerning ice in the area. They had been informed by Captain Smith that icebergs were usually present more to the north of their position, but at 9 am they had received a message from Cunard's RMS *Coronia* stating that they had seen: 'Bergs, growlers and field ice.' This was followed at 11.40 am by a warning from SS *Noordam,* which was also on its way to New York, simply stating that they had seen: 'Much ice.' At 1.42 pm RMS *Baltic* warned of: 'Icebergs, and large quantities of field ice.' At 7.30 pm Harold overheard a transmission from SS *Californian* to its fellow Leyland Line ship the SS *Antillian,* stating that they had seen: 'Three large bergs five miles to the southward of us.'

Harold Bride was concerned for his workmate and did not really sense any alarm:

> I remember how tired he [Phillips] was and got out of bed to relieve him. I didn't even feel the shock. I hardly knew it had happened until after the captain had come to us. There was no jolt whatsoever. I was standing by Phillips telling him to go to bed when the captain put his head into the cabin.
>
> 'We've struck an iceberg,' the captain said, 'and I'm having an inspection made to tell what it has done for us. You better get ready to send out a call for assistance. But don't send it until I tell you.'
>
> The captain went away, and in ten minutes, I should estimate the time, he came back. We could hear a terrible confusion outside, but there was not the least thing to indicate that there was any trouble. The wireless was working perfectly.
>
> 'Send the call for assistance,' said the captain, barely putting his head in the door.
>
> 'What call should I send?' asked Phillips.
>
> 'Send the regulation international call for help, just that.' Then the captain was gone.
>
> Phillips began to send 'C Q D' – he flashed away at it and we were joking while he did so. All of us made light of the disaster. We joked that way while he flashed signals for about five minutes. Then the captain came back.
>
> 'What are you sending?' he asked.
>
> 'C Q D,' Phillips replied.
>
> The humour of the situation appealed to me. I cut in with a little remark that made us all laugh, including the captain.
>
> 'Send S O S,' I said. 'It's the new call, and it may be your last chance to send it.'
>
> Phillips, with a laugh, changed the signal to S O S.'

Lawrence Beesley, a Yorkshireman who taught at a school in Dulwich, remembered some of the remarks made by the unsuspecting people after the collision:

> The general impression was that we had just scraped the iceberg with a glancing blow on the starboard side, and they had stopped as a wise precaution, to examine her thoroughly all over. 'I expect the iceberg has scratched off some of her new paint,' said one, 'and the captain doesn't like to go on until she is painted up again.' We

laughed at his estimate of the captain's care for the ship. Poor Captain Smith! – he knew by this time only too well what had happened.

According to sketches produced from the observations of Jack Thayer, the ship hit the iceberg at 12.45 am, and the lifeboats were ordered to be launched about twenty minutes later. As she sank, Titanic broke in half at about 1.40 am and the forward end sank soon afterwards. At 2 am, Jack Philips noted: 'Stern section pivots amidships and swings over spot where forward section sank.' The stern stayed upright for a short time and then plunged down into the water and was gone. No human eye would see it again for over seventy years.

The CS *Carpathia* was on its way from New York to Gibraltar and was fortunately in the region at the time of *Titanic*'s sinking. On receiving a distress signal, it immediately set a course towards the disaster area. After working through dangerous ice fields, the *Carpathia* arrived at the scene at 4 am on 15 April. Some people, mostly woman and children, had escaped from the ship in lifeboats and *Carpathia* saved over 700 of them.

SURVIVORS

Lifeboat number 7 was situated at the front of the ship on the starboard side, which happened to be the area above where the ship had hit the iceberg. It was the first to be launched, at about 12.40 am.

It is interesting to note that as lifeboat 7 was being rowed away from the stricken ship, quite nonchalantly, an actress named Helen Bishop suddenly remarked, 'We have to be rescued for the rest of my prophecy to come true.' The reason for the remark was that while she and her new husband were in Egypt, she had decided to visit a fortune teller. The seer divined her future, saying that she would survive a shipwreck, and an earthquake, before an automobile accident would end her life. Helen was pregnant at the time of the sinking, but she lost the baby only two days into its life – something the fortune teller appears to have failed to detect.

Lifeboat 5 was the second to be launched, at 12.45. By this time Bruce Ismay 'with his dressing gown and pyjamas on' was at the scene, and he shouted to Officer Pitman to, 'Hurry up; there is no time to waste! Fill the boat with women and children!' To which Pitman, not knowing who Ismay was, replied that he would await the captain's orders first. It eventually dawned on him who the man was, so Pitman went to the bridge and told the captain what he had suggested, and the captain told him to 'Carry on' – meaning to 'go ahead' with the suggestion.

On returning to lifeboat 5, Officer Pitman and Bruce Ismay helped several women and at least two children into the boat. Officer Murdoch came and told Officer Pitman to get into the boat, too, and to take charge of its evacuation, before asking him to try to stay around the right rear gangway door in case his boat was needed. First Officer Murdoch wished him well as he departed.

Annie Stengel had woken her husband Charles from a dream which was making him stir and moan. They felt a slight jarring of the ship, and became concerned when they realised that the engines had stopped. They went to investigate and were on A Deck when they saw Captain Smith come up from below looking very grave, which prompted Charles to remark that the situation might be serious. They climbed the stairs to the boat deck and Mrs Stengel got into lifeboat 5, wearing a kimono over her night dress, leaving Charles, who was not fully dressed, to walk forward towards the emergency lifeboat 1.

First Officer Murdoch gave Charles Stengel and another American businessman named Abram Salomon permission to get into emergency lifeboat 1. However, as Mr Stengel climbed over a waist-high railing, he stumbled and rolled into the boat, landing in an undignified heap and causing Mr Murdoch to laugh as he remarked, 'That is the funniest sight I have seen tonight.' However, Mr Stengel said that he took heart from the officer's reaction, which prompted him to think that things were not so bad after all. He was reunited with his wife when they both arrived on board *Carpathia*.

Charles Stengel was interviewed by the *Newark Star* and the *Newark Evening News* for 19 April 1912, giving them both detailed accounts:

> We retired about 10 o'clock. We had attended the concert and we knew that the captain was entertaining and dining his friends, among whom was Bruce Ismay, until 10 o'clock. Please say for me, in justice to Captain Smith, that he had not been drinking. He smoked cigarettes but he did not drink.
>
> I had been sleeping but a short time and was having a terrible dream which I cannot fully remember when I felt a shock. It was no greater than the one caused by the propeller coming above the

surface of the water. I thought, nevertheless, that I would go on deck and ascertain if there was any trouble. There I found but few persons. No one seemed to fear danger.

The first inkling I had of danger was when I saw the serious face of Captain Smith, as he talked to George Widener, of Philadelphia.

The first order was to put on the life preservers and to lower the boats – this merely as a precaution. Even then it was not thought that it would be necessary to use either. This was about midnight.

I cannot repeat too often that we thought the ship absolutely unsinkable. When we struck the iceberg, the portholes were open and some of the ice jammed through into the staterooms. One of the men picked up the ice and as he held it in his hand said smilingly, 'We must have struck an iceberg.' He had absolutely no thought of making any preparations to leave the ship.

The Titanic struck on her starboard side and her sides were ripped open where the coal bunkers are located. On the starboard side there was about six boats lowered. I do not know much about the other side. The women were put immediately into the boats. The wives were separated from their husbands, daughters from their fathers. Mrs Isidor Straus, rather than be separated from her husband, chose to die with him.

After Mrs Stengel had been lowered, I walked up toward the bow and saw them preparing to lower the light boats on which I finally put out to sea.

I saw Sir Cosmo Duff-Gordon and the rest of his party seated in the boat and saw there was room for one more. I asked the mate if I might get in. Even then I did not think that I was saving my life.

The boat was a high one and it was difficult for me to enter it. I finally managed to climb up, but was not very graceful in doing so. In fact, I rolled in, and the mate jokingly said, 'That is the funniest thing I have seen tonight.' I have not seen that mate [Fifth Officer Harold Lowe] since. The action of this officer proved to me conclusively that not even the crew were aware of the danger.

I wish you to emphatically say that Colonel John Jacob Astor was not threatened by any of the officers. The last seen of him he was calmly walking the upper deck. It was only after five men jumped into one of the boats that was meant to hold only women that the officer threatened to shoot the next man who showed himself a coward. To prove that he meant what he said he fired one shot into the air. This was sufficient to convince the men that the officer was in earnest. The lifeboats were absolutely unprepared for any emergencies. In fact, some of the so-called collapsible boats could not be opened. This caused the death of a number of persons.

> Another indication of the negligence of the steamship company was that two of the boats had no plugs in them when they were lowered. These boats are believed to have been lost. There was no food, no light, no compass and no water in any of the boats. We just trusted in God.
>
> My boat met with difficulty right from the start. Its painter was stuck fast, and it was only after considerable time had been spent that she was finally loosened and lowered.
>
> Some of the men ordered to man the boats proved themselves cowards. One Armenian wrapped himself in a blanket and refused absolutely to pull the oar. This boat was manned by two girls.

On *Carpathia*, Mr Stengel stated '...the reason there were so few press dispatches is because it was ruled by the authorities aboard the *Carpathia* that only twenty words of press could be sent each day. The wireless operators were told to send only the messages of those on board ship.'

The *New York Herald* for 26 April, reported: 'Mr Charles Stengel, of New York, describes the impact as terrific, tons of ice falling on the deck, and killing a number of men. The bows of the ship were torn asunder, and the water poured in, and pandemonium reigned. He pays a great tribute to the bravery displayed by the sailors and officers.'

In a letter he wrote on 3 May 1912, he stated:

> My experience on the *Titanic* was such as no one can realize the experience is often written about in books but very rarely experienced by people. Until I was allowed to get into a boat the suspense was fearful as my wife was in the second boat lowered and they only allowed women in the boats and with all were loaded that were around. It was only by luck I walked to the emergency boat which was away from the regular life saving boats. After being afloat for about an hour I saw the boilers explode and the ship go down. At that moment about 1,600 people jumped into the ocean and began to cry for help. This cry which was like a wail I will never forget. After floating for about five hours we were picked up by the 'Carpathia' and of course was relieved when I found my wife.

In an article in the *Sunday Express* for 20 November 1955, it was reported that as *Titanic* was sinking, 'Mr Stengel turned his back, stating, "I cannot look any longer."' Adding that he and Sir Cosmo: 'Did not get along very well.'

Eleanor Cassebeer stated that just after the collision 'things felt weird', and she became suspicious when she noticed that the lid of her trunk in cabin D-31 was not level and sensed that *Titanic* was leaning forward a bit. She met up with Harry Anderson, who escorted her to lifeboat 5.

On the night of the collision Mr and Mrs Kimball had actually reported that ice had entered their cabin through the porthole. As they started from their staterooms, orders were already being shouted to put on lifebelts. They did so as quickly as they could, and then made their way up to the boat deck. When Mrs Beckwith reached lifeboat 5, she asked Bruce Ismay if men could get in too. 'Certainly, madam,' Mr Ismay replied. Mr Ismay then called out, 'Are there any more to get into this boat?', but none appeared, so Karl Behr, the Beckwiths and the Kimballs all got in. Newspapers reported that Karl had proposed to Helen in the lifeboat.

In an interview with the *Brooklyn Daily Bugle*, Karl Behr remembered

> Mr Beckwith and I had stayed up in the card room while the women had retired at 11.30. We left the smoking room just before the closing for the night and I started to undress in my cabin. I felt a distinct jar, followed by a quivering of the boat. It was distinct to know we had hit something. I dressed and immediately went after my party, having clearly in my mind what course I would pursue. I met Miss Newsom in the passage, she having been awakened by the thud. We went together to the very upper deck and found it bitterly cold. The ship noticeably listed to starboard, the side which had been hit. I knew the boat was dangerously injured, although I could not then believe she was doomed. Together we went to the cabin of the Beckwiths, telling them to dress. Everybody put on warm clothes.
>
> When we were proceeding along the passage someone told us orders were issued to don lifebelts, which we did very calmly. We met Captain Smith on the main stairway and he was telling everyone to put on lifebelts. Knowing exactly where the lifeboats were, I led

my party to the uppermost deck. We waited quietly while one boat was filled [lifeboat 7]. It appeared to be comfortably occupied. We then went to the second boat [lifeboat 5], which had about forty in it. Mr Ismay himself directed the launching splendidly.

We were evidently the last passengers on the top deck. This was later explained by the fact that passengers were ordered to go to A Deck, while we had gone above that. There were other lifeboats on our side, but they must have been filled later from the lower decks. Our boat being lowered into the water, we rowed immediately away from the ship. We could only work four oars at a time on account of the somewhat cramped positions. We made good progress, however, and were soon a safe distance from the ship, which we still did not believe was going to sink. We stopped rowing when far enough out and transferred some of our passengers to another boat, probably the first one launched. The night was perfectly clear and all we could do was sit and wait. We had no idea of the number of lifeboats, and, although it only seemed a few minutes, it was two hours before the boat [*Titanic*] actually sank. The officer in charge of our boat [Third Officer Bert Pitman] seeing the men swimming in the water, refused to go back and I guess he was right, for he claimed we surely would have been swamped by the hundreds in the water.

What happened actually on board, of course, I saw little. No panic was evident and I heard no pistol shots. We floated around until dawn, when we saw the lights of the *Carpathia*, and started to row in her direction; as did all the lifeboats. The people aboard the *Carpathia* were fine, and officers, men and passengers cannot be praised too highly. They had made every preparation for our comfort. Quarters and clothes were generously distributed. Personally I am a little ****ived, but otherwise none the worse for the experience.

Karl Behr's party endured freezing weather, and lifeboats 5 and 7 did not drift too far away from each other throughout the dark hours. They were the third and fourth boats to be rescued by *Carpathia*.

Lifeboat 3 became the third vessel launched from the starboard forward section of the ship. This vessel had similar problems to that which lifeboat 7 had suffered, descending in fits and starts, as the lowering ropes became stuck in the pulleys, but it eventually it reached the water.

First Officer Murdoch and Fifth Officer Lowe supervised the action. Officer Lowe remembered that when he reached the boat deck: 'I could feel by my feet there was something wrong – it is not listing it is tipping – she was by the bow; she was very much by the bow. She had a grade downhill ... by the head.'

After Harry Anderson had put Eleanor Cassebeer in lifeboat 5, he took a place in lifeboat 3. It seems that some of the bored passengers argued with each other as the freezing night went on, and they were rescued by *Carpathia* at about 7.30 am.

Also in lifeboat 3 was first class passenger Adolf Saalfeld. He was a self-made businessman who had brought on board with him a black leather satchel containing sixty-five small glass vials of various perfume fragrances, which he intended to take to America to take advantage of the large expanding market there. They seem to be the fragrances that were popular in the Edwardian period such as Lily of the Valley, Blushing Rose and Orange Blossom. They were lost in the sinking, but all but three were retrieved from the Titanic wreck in 2000.

It was now approaching 1 am. Quartermaster George Rowe had been on duty on the poop deck, where he saw a mass of ice pass by very close to the starboard side of the ship. He noticed a lifeboat had been launched in that vicinity. He was asked to collect some distress rockets and take them up to the bridge. On arriving he was met by Officer Joseph Boxhall, and they both began the task of firing off the flares.

Officer Boxhall noted, 'Every time I fired a signal I had to clear everybody away from the vicinity of the rocket.' He remembered that he was sending rockets up right until the time Captain Smith told him to leave off sending up the flares and to get into emergency lifeboat 2 and take charge.

Emergency lifeboat 1 was the front vessel of the four on the starboard side, and was the fourth and last to be launched by officers Murdoch and Lowe, at about 1.05 am, and Lookout George Symons was placed in charge. It had a capacity for forty people but only twelve eventually got in; the fewest to escape in any single lifeboat that night. It prompted a greaser who was standing at a lower deck named Wally Hurst to remark, 'If they are sending the boats away they might as well put some people in them.'

Lady Duff-Gordon's secretary, London-born Laura Mabel 'Franks' Francatelli, had been woken when she realised there was water seeping under her cabin door, and dashed up to alert the Duff-Gordons, who were sleeping in separate cabins. Lucy was aware there was a problem because she had heard a noise: 'It seemed almost like people playing bowls, rolling the great balls along, and the ship stopped.'

The ladies put on as much clothing as they could, and Sir Cosmo grabbed a flask of brandy, his automatic pistol, and a handful of cigars, which he later handed out to the seamen in the lifeboat. When the trio came out onto the boat deck, they were also wearing their life-preservers, which all must have been very cumbersome. Franks remembered: 'I then noticed that the sea was nearer to us than during the day.' She stated to Sir Cosmo, 'We are sinking.' To which he replied, 'Nonsense, come away.'

Lady Duff-Gordon and Franks were asked several times to get into one of the three lifeboats that had been loaded and launched on the starboard front of the ship, but they refused because they did not want to leave Sir Cosmo to his fate. Eventually, they were offered seats in emergency lifeboat 1, and Franks recalled, 'There were no other women there by that time. The officer saw us and ordered us in, and we said we would go if Sir Cosmo could come also.' The officer decided to allow all three to get in. Despite the 'women and children first' drill, Officer Lowe allowed seven male members of the crew and only five passengers to get into the lifeboat, of which only two were women – Lady Duff-Gordon and Franks.

When the lifeboat had descended to about B Deck it encountered a spar, an obstacle such as a piece of rigging sticking out like a pole from the side of the ship, which became trapped under the gunwale (the piece of metal fitted around the top of the boat to strengthen it) and the procedure was stopped abruptly. The crew had to cut at the obstacle with wire cutters to free the craft, and it did not reach the water until about 1.15 am. Officers shouted down to them a last instruction that they should row away from the ship as fast as they could, and having seven crew members in the boat it was not long before they had rowed some distance away.

While in the lifeboat, some of the crew talked about how they had lost their kits and would have their pay stopped from the time the ship was wrecked. Sir Cosmo or Lady Gordon overheard them and replied, 'We will give you a little to start a new kit.'

On the following day Sir Cosmo kept to his word and paid the crew members £5 ($20) each – now worth over £300 – which he stated was to help to replace their uniforms and kit, and to help them and their families financially. Some, mainly in the Media, have described the gift as blood money for saving their lives, but why would Sir Cosmo pay them a bribe after he had been saved? The promissory note presented to Able Seaman Albert Horswill still exists.

Lady Duff-Gordon's story was published in the *Daily News* for 21 April 1912, in which she stated:

> 'I was asleep when the crash occurred. I had previously been watching the fields of ice, and an officer had pointed out to us one monster which was apparently 100 feet high, and several miles long. I was awakened by a long, grinding crash, and aroused my husband. He ran to investigate the cause, and returning, said to me. 'We have hit a big berg.' We then adjusted our life preservers, and went on deck.
>
> There was no excitement at this time. The ship was listed slightly, but nobody dreaded any serious result. They did not think that she could sink. There was little alarm even when the officers came running amongst us, saying that the women and children must go to the boats. It was thought that only ordinary precautions necessary in the case were being taken.
>
> Our boat was the 12th or 13th to be launched. It contained five stokers, two Americans named Solomon and Stengel, two sailors,

my husband, myself, and Miss Frank, an English girl. Numbers of men who were standing nearby when our boat was launched joked with us because we were going out on to the ocean, and said, 'You'll get your death of cold out there amid the ice.' We cruised around for two hours, and suddenly saw the *Titanic* give a curious shiver. There were no lights on the ship, except for a few lanterns.

We heard several pistol shots, and a great screaming from the decks. The stern lifted high in the air as a tremendous explosion occurred. Then there was another explosion, and the whole forward part of the great steamer went under. The stern at the same time rose still higher, till it was 100 feet in the air like and enormous black figure against the sky. What appeared to be little figures hung for a moment at the rearmost portion of the great black mass, and then dropped into the water. The screaming from the ship was agonising. I never heard such a continued chorus of utter agony.

A minute or two later the *Titanic*'s stern slowly disappeared as though a great hand was pushing it gently under the waves. As it sank, the screaming of some poor souls aboard seemed to grow louder. At this time we lay 200 yards away, watching. We saw her go down slowly, and almost peacefully. When the stern disappeared, there was for one moment an awful silence. Then from the water where the *Titanic* had been arose a bedlam of shrieks and cries from women and men clinging to the wreckage in the icy water.

It was at least an hour before that awful chorus ceased, gradually dying from the loud shrieks and cries down into a moan of despair. The last despairing cry I heard was in a man's voice.

'My God! My God!' he repeated monotonously, and in a dull, hopeless way. Then it ceased, and in place of that awful dying chorus there was the silence of death.

One iceberg, possibly the one which the *Titanic* struck, seemed to pursue our boat, and to threaten to crush us. Our rowers made frantic efforts to get past it in safety, and succeeded in keeping clear.

At last the morning came, and with the light we were horrified to see on the one side, as far as the eye could reach, a succession of ice-floes and big bergs, and on the other a school of tremendous whales. Then, when we seemed beset with danger on both sides, we caught sight of the *Carpathia* looming up in the distance, and heading straight for us. We were too numb with horror or with cold to utter a sound.

There were more than 50 women who had lost their husbands, including brides, when we assembled on the deck of the *Carpathia*. The gloom amongst us was ghastly. I buried myself in the cabin, and did not come on to the deck again until we reached New York.

Despite the problems they had when launching the lifeboat, it was a lighter craft, so the Duff-Gordons were rescued by *Carpathia* at about 4.30 am, a relatively short time out on the sea, and only emergency lifeboat 2 from the portside had reached the rescue ship previously.

The next lifeboats to be launched were situated at the portside front of the ship. Officer Lightoller was by lifeboat 6 when he noticed: '... she [the ship] was distinctly down by the head, and I think it was while working at that boat it was noticed she had a pretty heavy list to port.' He continued, 'However, having got Captain Smith's sanction, I indicated to the Bosun's Mate [Albert Haines], and we lowered down the first boat [number 6 at 1.10 am] down to the boat deck, and, just at this time, thank heaven, the frightful din of the escaping steam suddenly stopped, and there was a death-like silence.'

Quartermaster Hichens was ordered by Officer Lightoller to get in the lifeboat and take charge. As the boat was being lowered, Hichens shouted back up to the boat deck that the boat was badly manned. Officer Lightoller called for assistance from anyone who had experience of the sea and Major Peuchen stepped forward and offered his services, stating his experience as a yachtsman. Captain Smith suggested that the major should go down to the promenade deck so he could break a window and access the boat from there, but Officer Lightoller was of the opinion that if he was as good a sailor as he claimed, he should be capable of sliding down the ropes to get into the boat. Major Peuchen then grabbed a rope and climbed down hand-over-hand to the boat.

With the headline, 'This Boat Can't Sink', the *Perth Daily News* for 28 May 1912, reported:

> Major Arthur Peuchen, of Toronto, said; 'We were all pleased with the trip until the crash. After a few minutes following the collision, I went to my friends and said that it was not serious.
>
> 'Fifteen minutes later I met Mr Charles Hays of the Grand Trunk Railway. I asked him, "Have you seen the ice?" and I took him up

> and showed him it. Then I noticed that the boat was listing, and I said to Mr Hays, "She's listing. She should not do that." He said, "Oh, I don't know, this boat can't sink." He had a good deal of confidence, and said, "It does not matter what we've struck, she is good for eight or ten hours.
>
> 'I went back to the cabin deck where I met men and women coming up. The boats were being prepared for lowering on the port side. Women came forward one by one accompanied by their husbands. They would only allow women to pass, and the men had to stand back. The second officer [Lightoller] stood there and that was the order enforced. Two men passengers got into the boat.
>
> 'I was surprised that the sailors were not at their posts as they should have been. I've seen fire drills, and the action of the sailors did not impress me. They seemed to be short of sailors round the lifeboats where I was.
>
> 'When I came on deck first it seemed to me that about 100 stokers came up and crowded the deck. One of the officers, a splendid man, drove these men off the deck like sheep. When we got to the next boat a quartermaster and a sailor were put in, and the boat was then filled with women. We called out for more women. Some would not leave their husbands.
>
> 'The second boat was lowered, and, as it was going down, the second officer said, "I can't manage this boat with only one seaman."
>
> 'I was standing by and said, "Can I be of any assistance? I'm a yachtsman."
>
> 'He replied, "Yes, I would rather have you than a sailor."
>
> 'I got hold of a rope and lowered myself into the boat. We got the rudder in and I took an oar with a sailor. We were told to row away as fast as we could to get clear of the suction.'

When he first went out of his cabin to find out what had happened, Arthur Peuchen left $200,000-worth of securities in his cabin, and the money went down with the ship.

Also in lifeboat 6 were mother and daughter Elsie and Edith Bowerman, who were active suffragettes and friends of Emmeline Pankhurst. As recently as Saturday, 6 April 1912, Elsie had attended an open-air meeting of suffragettes in Hastings, to support the cause. Elsie wrote, 'The silence when the engines stopped was followed by a steward knocking on the door and telling us to go up on deck. This we did and were lowered into lifeboats, when we were told to get away from the liner as soon as we could because of suction. This we did, and to pull an oar in the midst of the Atlantic in April with icebergs floating about is a strange experience.'

Several passengers made none too complimentary remarks about Quartermaster Hichens' behaviour in the lifeboat, including Leila Meyer, who accused him of being drunk. In his defence he stated:

> I would like to make a little statement as regarding Mrs Meyer's statement in the newspapers about my drinking the whisky, sir, and about the blankets. I was very cold, sir, and I was standing up in the boat. I had no hat on. A lady had a flask of whisky or brandy, or something of that description, given her by some gentleman on the ship before she left, and she pulled it out and gave me about a tablespoonful and I drank it. Another lady, who was lying in the bottom of the boat, in a rather weak condition, gave me a half wet and half dry blanket to try keeping myself a little warm, as I was half frozen. I think it was very unkind of her, sir, to make any statement criticizing me. When we got to the ship I handled everyone as carefully as I could, and I was the last one to leave the boat, and I do not think I deserve anything like that to be put in the papers. That is what upset me and got on my nerves.

The next vessel to be launched from the portside front by officers Wilde and Lightoller was lifeboat 8 at 1 am, with Captain Smith also lending a hand. Emergency lifeboat 2 was launched by officers Wilde and Boxhall at about 1.40 am, or just after; with the operation being again overseen by Captain Smith. Lifeboat 9 was the first to be launched from the starboard rear of the vessel, by First Officer Murdoch and Sixth Officer James Moody at about 1.15 am. They were assisted by Purser McElroy and Mr Ismay.

James Widgery had completed an inspection of the swimming facility before going to bed at 10 pm. On being wakened by his room-mates, he had arrived at his assigned position at lifeboat 7, but it was already being launched when he got there. Purser McElroy told him and a saloon steward named William Ward to accompany him to the back of the ship to assist with the loading and launching of lifeboat 9. Widgery was given a box of biscuits by a store man to be placed in the boat, and as he was doing so Mr McElroy asked him if he understood anything about lifeboats. When he replied that he knew a little, he was told to stay in the boat to help with the rowing.

After launching lifeboat 9, Officer Murdoch and Moody moved on to deal with lifeboat 11, which they launched at 1:20 am. Ten minutes later, at about 1.30, Murdoch and Moody moved quickly on to prepare lifeboat 13 for launching.

It would seem that only five minutes had elapsed before Murdoch and Moody had moved quickly on from lifeboat 13 to prepare lifeboat 15 for launching; the fourth and final lifeboat at the starboard rear of the ship. This was the fourth lifeboat the same two officers had prepared and launched together, and by this time they must have been tired and feeling the strain.

Frank Dymond had been on his way to start his shift when he discovered that the door to the boiler room was shut and the stairwell was flooded. He was assigned to lifeboat 15, but when he got up to the starboard rear of the boat deck, he saw that lifeboats 13 and 15 had already been prepared for launching. Instead, he was told to get into lifeboat 15 and ordered to take charge.

Under the heading 'Stories of Survivors at Plymouth – Frank Dymond', the *Western Times* for 30 April 1912, reported on what it seems Frank had recited to a reporter:

> A fireman named Dymond, of Southampton, related that on the day preceding the disaster, the *Titanic* was proceeding at 22 and a half knots and had entered the iceberg zone. The sea was as calm and still as a pond, and the day was fine and with sunshine. Small clumps of ice could be seen in all directions, but there was no indication of large floes, or bergs. The crew and passengers were calculating on a most enjoyable trip in probably record time. This fact was gathered by the general conversations carried on all hands.
>
> Most of the passengers had retired by 11.30 pm and there were only a few moving about the vessel, enjoying the quietness of the scene, which was of an inspiring character. Mr Dymond had just

looked at his watch, which indicated twenty minutes to midnight, when he heard a sound similar to a knife being drawn over a rasp. He ran up on deck to see what the matter was. No harm seemed to have been done, so he went back to the stokehold again.

It was not long however before water started to pour in, and it had reached his ankles when he saw that something serious must have happened. He was then about to come off duty.

When he came on deck again he saw the boats being told off. In fact, they had all but one left the side of the vessel. He was told off to man his boat [lifeboat 15], but just as he was getting into her something happened, and he was swept on one side. There was no eagerness to get into the boat; however, the difficulty really was to get sufficient persons to go away in her.

He was again warned off to man the boat, and this time he took his place. Eventually there were 68 souls aboard this boat. There were no sailors. So far as he could see there was a deal of confusion, and scores who had first chance to get into the boats preferred to remain on the ship.

Dymond says he was ordered to stand by for a time, and when there was no response to the repeated call, 'Any more women to go?' he was told to fill up the boat and get away. Six or seven hours later the boat was rescued by *Carpathia*.

Under the headings 'Ex-Navy Man in Charge Tells his Story – 68 in Leaking Boat', Dymond's account published in the *Daily Mirror* for 7 May 1912, differs in some sections from the previous report:

Our boat had been damaged by striking the ship's gunwale when we were first lowered. The men on the second deck had to step across about two feet from the rail to the side of the boat.

There was a rush. Men clambered across anyhow. I saw we were full up and I called out loudly, 'Lower Away!' Three men fell into the sea, and one foreigner I had to hit as he jumped and he too fell.

Fred Barrett called up from boat 13 below us, 'Stop lowering, or you will swamp us.' I shouted this to the men above and we stopped six feet from the water. Number 13 got clear, and we dropped with a splash. We all got wet, and some water came into the boat.

The current drifted us under the propellers of the *Titanic*, which were sticking up in the air. She drew 33 feet of water, and her keel at the stern was 12 feet above our heads. It had taken us an hour to get the boat away, and was than about half-past-one. We drifted about 300 yards away.

There had been a lot of trouble keeping men out of the boat before she left the boat deck. A foreigner came up with a child in his arms, and we tried to get the child from him to put in the boat, but he would not give it up. At last we took him in too. We did not know till afterwards that it was his child.

I had a tussle with a man who had two lifebelts on the ship's deck. I had to stretch him out and take one away from him to give to a little Irishman who had none at all.

There were 68 people in the boat, including six other men from the stock-hold and me. I was the only Navy man and so I took command. It was fortunate I was there, for I found the plug and put it in, and made them all sit still.

We had to move very carefully, for the gunwales were never more than six inches above the water, and she was leaking on one side just about the water level, where she had been bumped on the ship's gunwale. We were only able to get at five of the eight oars, and the men only rowed to keep warm. I had my left hand on the tiller, and could not move to use my right instead. Noss [Fireman Henry Noss] sometimes relieved me with his left hand. Even now my left hand goes numb sometimes. I could not feel with it on the *Carpathia*.

I had nothing on at all but a flannel sweater and dungaree pants. A spare sweater I had tucked in my belt I gave to a little trimmer named Fredericks beside me to put round his neck. Fred Barrett in 13 was the same.

It was bitter cold. The water was one degree below freezing point, and the air was colder. We had been in the water about fifteen minutes when the first explosion occurred. That was what finished her. If she had broken in two and the after part would have floated, for she was not ripped all along by the collision.

The stern came down after the first explosion, and fifteen minutes later came another explosion, which must have been her aft boilers, for the stern went right up and all the lights went out.

Then we heard the most awful noise one could possibly hear. The machinery shifted with a grinding roar, and there were dreadful shrieks and cries on board and around her in the sea. And then, about fifteen minutes later, and forty-five minutes from the time we entered the water, she plunged.

There was one 'Dago' in the boat who kept crying out, 'We are lost! We shall all be drowned!' and if I could have reached him could have brained him with the tiller, for he was scaring the women. The rest of the men were quiet. I made the women sit as low as possible in the boat to shelter them.

Even when [lifeboat] 15 was in the water I did not believe the ship would sink altogether.

One of the pleasantest things I remember is what a little Irish girl said to me in the boat. 'It's like this, sir', she said, she called me sir because I was in command – 'We know we are along with Englishmen, and we know that we will get saved if there is a chance.'

We burnt shirts, handkerchiefs, rags and bits of flannel raised up on the boat hook. There were plenty of matches in the men's pockets, but the rags only smouldered after the first blaze. A few men smoked cigarettes they had in their pockets.

From about 1.20 am Chief Officer Wilde and officers Lightoller, Lowe and Moody began working on lifeboats 10, 12, 14 and 16 at the rear of the ship on the left (port) side, which had become the danger zone, as passengers and some of the crew had realised *Titanic* was going down and their chances of survival were slim.

Saloon Steward Charles Andrews escaped in lifeboat 16. He stated:

'I came off watch about a quarter to 11 and went down and turned in. About 20 minutes after that I was wakened up by a movement of the ship, and I heard the rush of water. Several of the boys woke up with the shock also. So with that I got out of my bunk and went into the working alleyway, seeing lots of stewards out. I walked up and down the alleyway several times with another steward. After that I went back to the quarters. I went back and lay down for a few minutes and then got up again. I had no sooner gotten there than somebody came and said, 'All hands on deck'.

I walked up on deck and stood by my boat. There were lots of people around, and I saw stores brought to the boat, and bread. I did not see the stores put in the boat. I assisted in helping the ladies and children into the boat. After the boat was full the officer called out for able-seamen, or any individuals then, to man the boat.

I should think there were about fifty passengers. There was no effort on the part of the steerage men to get into our boat. I was told by the officer to allow none in it. When the officer started to fill the boat with passengers, and the men to man it, there were no individuals who tried to get in, or that he permitted to get in. There was no confusion whatever. After they were all in the boat the officer looked around at me and asked me if I could take an oar, and I said I could, sir. At that he told me to get into the boat. After I got in the boat I assisted by putting the rowlocks in. We lowered the boat to the water and rowed away from the ship. On our way out we … had

> to rest because we came across another boat, sir, filled up with ladies. The remark was passed by someone in the boat to go back, but as the two boats were full we stood at a distance away.

Officers Wilde and Lightoller began to work on launching lifeboat 12 at about 1.25 am, and lifeboat 14 was launched at 1.30 am, by officers Wilde, Lightoller, Lowe and Moody. Officer Lowe eventually got into lifeboat 14 and took charge.

Lifeboat 14's descent was stopped at A Deck and the crew shouted out if there were any women and children in the area, but there was no reply. As the descent continued, Officer Lowe was forced to fire two bullets down the side of the ship, which splashed into the water below, in an effort to warn any more individuals from trying to get in.

Then there was another problem, as Able Seaman Scarrott recalled: 'The aft fall got twisted and we dropped the boat by releasing gear and when the boat was in the water we rowed clear of the ship.' Apparently, the problem caused a leak and water started pouring into the lifeboat.

He continued:

> The sight of that grand ship going down will never be forgotten. She slowly went down bow first with a slight list to starboard until the water reached the bridge then she went quicker. When the third funnel had nearly disappeared I heard four explosions, which I took to be the bursting of the boilers. The ship was right up on end then. Suddenly she broke in two between the third and fourth funnel. The after part of the ship came down on the water in its normal position and seemed as if it was going to remain afloat, but it only remained a minute or two and then sank. The lights were burning right up until she broke in two. The cries from the poor souls struggling in the water seemed terrible in the stillness of the night. It seemed to go through you like a knife.

About 150 yards from where *Titanic* sank, they came upon lifeboats 4, 10 and 12. They were all filled mostly with women and children, but there was no officer in charge of them. Officer Lowe wanted to go back to the wreck site to see if he could save any people from the water, so he decided to take charge of them all, and he strung them all together. He thought that they would make a larger object to be seen from a passing ship.

Included in these three lifeboats were Charles Williams, Marian Thayer and the Carter and Ryerson families in lifeboat 4; and the Fortune family in lifeboat 10.

Officer Lightoller had dropped lifeboat 4 to A Deck, which was one below the boat deck, with the intention of loading from there. However, the windows were locked and he could not load at first, so he left the vessel dangling where it was with the intention of returning to it later, which he did at about 1.50 am.

Charles Williams had been playing in the squash court until 10.30 pm and was resting in the smoking room when the collision occurred. He saw the iceberg and estimated that it rose a hundred feet above the deck; before it broke up about mid-ships and drifted away into the darkness. He was wearing a life preserver when he jumped from the starboard boat deck and tried to get as far away from the ship as he could. He stated that he had to stand up in the first lifeboat he got into, and Marian Thayer confirmed that she also had to stand up in lifeboat 4, so this may have been the first lifeboat he entered.

Charles spoke of his ordeal to George E. Standing, who in turn told the *New York World*:

> He [Charles Williams] is a good swimmer, and went overboard with a life preserver when he couldn't stay on deck any longer. He was in the icy water for over two hours before he was finally hauled into one of the lifeboats. He says that he saw Captain Smith swimming around in the icy water with an infant in his arms and a lifebelt. When the small boat went to his rescue Captain Smith handed them the child, but refused to get in himself.

He was eventually transferred to lifeboat 14 and went back with Officer Lowe to try to pick up survivors, and because of the confusion in changing from lifeboat 4 to 14, it was originally reported that Charles had been lost in the sinking.

Lucile Polk Carter left a brief diary in which she tells of how she and William spent the time in the swimming baths and playing with their dogs; a King Charles spaniel and an Airedale Terrier.

After the dinner party in the à la carte restaurant, the ladies retired and the men played cards in the first-class smoking room, where Willie Carter was when the ship stopped. He went to his cabin and told Lucile to get dressed and head up to the top deck. When they got there Lucile, Miss Serreplaa and the two children got into lifeboat 4.

Lucile remembered that there were no seamen in the boat, and realising it was a life or death situation, she grabbed an oar, and some of the other women followed suit. She recalled:

> She was sinking, and we were warned by cries from the men above to pull away from the ship quickly. Mrs Thayer ... was in my boat, and she too took an oar. It was cold and we had no time to clothe ourselves with warm overcoats. The rowing warmed me. We started to pull away from the ship. We could see the dim outlines of the decks above, but we could not recognise anybody. I arrived at the *Carpathia* at 8 o'clock next morning, when I saw him [Mr Carter] leaning on the rail. All he said was that he had had a jolly good breakfast and that he never thought I would make it.

The Thayers had spent the day walking around the decks, taking time to talk to Bruce Ismay and Thomas Andrews, among others. Later, as Jack was having a coffee after dinner, he became acquainted with a man in his late twenties named Milton Long, and they chatted for a while. Eventually they all retired to their cabins.

They were all getting ready for bed when the collision occurred. Young Jack went on deck in his overcoat and slippers to investigate 'the fun' both at the front and at the back of the vessel, where he saw some ice. He returned to inform his parents what he had seen. His father accompanied him back on deck, and when they realised the ship was beginning to list, they went back to their cabins and put on warmer clothes and lifejackets.

They searched the top decks to try to find out what had happened, and as they did so, 'We saw, as they passed, Mr Ismay, Mr Andrews, and some of the ship's officers. Mr Andrews told us he did not give the ship much over an hour to live. We could hardly believe it, and yet if he said so it must be true. No one was better qualified to know.'

They went back to the stateroom to collect Marian and Margaret, the maid, and after making sure they had enough clothes on to keep warm they all went back up to A Deck, where they were joined by Milton Long. Marian and Margaret were ordered to the other side of the boat, but they were all reunited a little later. On being told that they were loading the forward boats on the port side from the deck below, they made their way to that deck. They suddenly found themselves in the thick of all the confusion, and Jack lamented, 'The lounge on B Deck was filled with a milling crowd, and as we went through the doorway onto the deck, people pushed between my father and mother and Long and me. Long and I could not catch up and were entirely separated from them. I never saw my father again.' Marian and Margaret eventually got into lifeboat 4.

Marian remembered:

> The after part of the ship then reared in the air, with the stern upwards, until it assumed an almost vertical position. It seemed to remain stationary in this position for many seconds (perhaps twenty), then suddenly dove straight down out of sight. It was 2.20 am when the *Titanic* disappeared, according to a wristwatch worn by one of the passengers in my boat.
>
> We pulled back to where the vessel had sunk and on our way picked up six men who were swimming – two of whom were drunk and gave us much trouble all the time. The six men picked up were hauled into the boat by women. Two of these men died in the boat.

> The boat we were in started to take on water; I do not know how. We had to bail. I was standing in ice-cold water up to the top of my boots all the time, and rowing continuously for nearly five hours. We took off about fifteen more people who were standing on a capsized boat. In all, our boat had by that time sixty-five or sixty-six people. There was no room to sit down in our boat, so we all stood, except some sitting along the side. I think the steerage passengers had as good a chance of the rest of us to be saved.
>
> The boat I was in was picked up by the *Carpathia* at 7.00 am on Monday, we having rowed three miles to her, as we could not wait to come up on account of our boat taking in so much water that we would not have stayed afloat much longer.
>
> I never saw greater courage or efficiency than was displayed by the officers of the ship. They were calm polite and perfectly splendid. They also worked hard. The bedroom stewards also behaved extremely well.

Jack Thayer and Milton Long eventually found themselves staring over the rail on the starboard side of the boat deck, close to the second funnel, with the freezing sea water beginning to engulf the ship and drag it down. As he was a good swimmer, Jack proposed that he and Milton Long should jump off the ship, but, after looking how far the drop was down to the water, Mr Long went against the idea. However, when the ship lunged forward dramatically, they agreed to attempt the task.

Jack recalled:

> We had no time to think now, only act. We shook hands, wished each other luck. I said, 'Go ahead; I'll be right with you.' I threw my overcoat off as he [Long] climbed over the rail, sliding down facing the ship. Ten seconds later I sat on the rail. I faced out, and with a push of my arms and hands, jumped into the water as far out from the ship as I could. When we jumped we were only 12 or 15 feet above the water – I never saw Long again.

Milton Long had perished.

Jack recalled that the cold was terrific, and that his watch had stopped at 2.22 am. After a dreadful struggle in the water, he finally made it to the upturned lifeboat collapsible B. He remembered the shouts from those who had been thrown into the icy water as, 'One long continuous wailing chant. It sounded like locusts on a midsummer night in the woods.'

After suffering a terrifying ordeal clinging for their lives on the ocean, Officer Lightoller blew a whistle to try to attract assistance, and they were eventually rescued by lifeboats 4 and 12. Jack got into lifeboat 12, but because of the dark and the distressing situation he was not aware that his mother was in the other boat. When Jack got to the *Carpathia* at 7.30 am he saw his mother, and when he got to the top of the ladder she asked, 'Where's Daddy?' He told her that he did not know. 'The journey of the next three days was one of crushing sorrow... It seemed as if there were none but widows left, each one mourning the loss of her husband. It was a most pitiful sight.'

While he was on board *Carpathia,* Jack described to an American named Lewis Skidmore how he saw *Titanic* as she sank and Mr Skidmore drew sketches based on his description. Collapsible B was eventually found floating in the sea and was recovered by the CS *Mackay-Bennett*. The sketches were used by Robert Ballard when trying to locate the wreck of the *Titanic* in the 1980s.

Arthur Ryerson stayed on the deck while his wife, his two daughters, and his son got into lifeboat 4. However, when Officer Lightoller saw John Borie in the boat, he tried to remove him, but Arthur pointed out that he was just a boy and the officer allowed him to stay. Officer Lightoller was strict in enforcing the 'women and children first' rule so it may be that he was aware that the Ryersons were on their way back to America, having already lost one of their sons; which is why he relented.

In later life, Jack Ryerson recalled how Officer Lightoller had called out that he could not enter one of the last lifeboats into which his mother, sisters and two female servants were boarding. It seems to have appeared to Lightoller that Jack looked old enough to remain behind with the men. His father stepped forward and argued that his son was only 13 and should be permitted to join his mother in the boat. The last Jack saw of his father was him standing with some acquaintances, looking very calm, as the lifeboat pulled away, and he never forgot how his father had saved his life.

In an affidavit sent to the Senate Inquiry, which was read out on 6 May 1912 (Day 16), Emily Borie Ryerson, gave the following evidence:

> At the time of collision I was awake and heard the engines stop, but felt no jar. My husband was asleep, so I rang and asked the steward, Bishop, what was the matter? He said, 'There is talk of an iceberg, ma'am, and they have stopped, not to run into it.' I told him to keep me informed if there were any orders. It was bitterly cold, so I put on a warm wrapper and looked out the window (we were in the large cabins on the B deck, very far aft) and saw the stars shining and a calm sea, but heard no noise. It was 12 o'clock. After about 10 minutes I went out in the corridor, and saw far off people hurrying on deck. A passenger ran by and called out, 'Put on your lifebelts and come up on the boat deck.'
>
> I said, 'Where did you get those orders?' He said, 'From the captain.' I went back then and told Miss Bowen and my daughter in the next room, to dress immediately, roused my husband and the two younger children, who were in a room on the other side, and then remembered my maid, who had a room near us. Her door was locked and I had some difficulty in waking her. By this time my husband was fully dressed, and we could hear the noise of feet tramping on the deck overhead. He was quite calm and cheerful and helped me put the lifebelts on the children and on my maid. I was paralyzed with fear of not all getting on deck together in time, as there were seven of us. I would not let my younger daughter dress, but she only put on a fur coat, as I did over her nightgown. My husband cautioned us all to keep together, and we went up to A deck, where we found quite a group of people we knew. Everyone had on a lifebelt, and they all were very quiet and self-possessed.
>
> We stood about there for quite a long time – fully half an hour, I should say. I know my maid ran down to the cabin and got some of my clothes. Then we were ordered to the boat deck. I only remember the second steward at the head of the stairs, who told us where to go. My chief thought and that of everyone else was, I know, not to make a fuss and to do as we were told. My husband joked with some of the women he knew, and I heard him say, 'Don't you hear the band

playing?' I begged him to let me stay with him, but he said, 'You must obey orders. When they say, "Women and children to the boats" you must go when your turn comes. I'll stay with John Thayer. We will be all right. You take a boat going to New York.' This referred to the belief that there was a circle of ships around waiting. The *Olympic*, the *Baltic*, were some of the names I heard.

All this time we could hear the rockets going up – signals of distress. Again, we were ordered down to A deck, which was partly enclosed. We saw people getting into boats, but waited our turn. There was a rough sort of steps constructed to get up to the window. My boy, Jack, was with me. An officer at the window said, 'That boy can't go.' My husband stepped forward and said, 'Of course, that boy goes with his mother; he is only 13.' So they let him pass. They also said, 'No more boys.' I turned and kissed my husband, and as we left, he and the other men I knew – Mr Thayer, Mr Widener, and others – were all standing there together very quietly. The decks were lighted, and as you went through the window it was as if you stepped out into the dark. We were flung into the boats. There were two men – an officer inside and a sailor outside – to help us. I fell on top of the women who were already in the boat, and scrambled to the bow with my eldest daughter. Miss Bowen and my boy were in the stern and my second daughter was in the middle of the boat with my maid. Mrs Thayer, Mrs Widener, Mrs Astor and Miss Eustis were the only others I knew in our boat.

Presently an officer called out from the upper deck, 'How many women are there in that boat?' Someone answered, 'Twenty-four.' 'That's enough; lower away.'

The ropes seemed to stick at one end and the boat tipped, someone called for a knife, but it was not needed until we got into the water, as it was but a short distance, and I then realized for the first time how far the ship had sunk. The deck we left was only about 20 feet from the sea. I could see all the portholes open and water washing in, and the decks still lighted.

Then they called out, 'How many seamen have you,' and they answered one. 'That is not enough,' said the officer, 'I will send you another,' and he sent a sailor down the rope. In a few minutes after several other men not sailors came down the ropes over the davits and dropped into our boat. The order was given to pull away, then they rowed off – the sailors, the women, anyone – but made little progress; there was a confusion of orders; we rowed toward the stern, someone shouted something about a gangway, and no one seemed to know what to do. Barrels and chairs were being thrown overboard.

Then suddenly, when we still seemed very near, we saw the ship was sinking rapidly. I was in the bow of the boat with my daughter and turned to see the great ship take a plunge toward the bow, the two forward funnels seemed to lean and then she seemed to break in half as if cut with a knife, and as the bow went under the lights went out; the stern stood up for several minutes, black against the stars, and then that, too, plunged down, and there was no sound for what seemed like hours, and then began the cries for help of people drowning all around us, which seemed to go on forever.

Someone called out, 'Pull for your lives, or you'll be sucked under,' and everyone that could row did so like mad. I could see my younger daughter and Mrs Thayer and Mrs Astor rowing, but there seemed to be no suction. Then we turned to pick up some of those in the water. Some of the women protested, but others persisted, and we dragged in six or seven men; the men we rescued were principally stokers, stewards, sailors, etc., and were so chilled and frozen already they could hardly move. Two of them died in the stern later and many were raving and moaning and delirious most of the time.

We had no lights or compass. There were several babies in the boat, but there was no milk or water. (I believe these were all stowed away somewhere, but no one knew where, and as the bottom of the boat was full of water and the boat full of people it was very difficult to find anything.)

After the *Titanic* sank we saw no lights, and no one seemed to know what direction to take. Lowe, the officer in charge of the boat, had called out earlier for all to tie together, so we now heard his whistle, and as soon as we could make out the other boats in the dark, five of us were tied together, and we drifted about without rowing, as the sea was calm, waiting for the dawn. It was very cold, and soon a breeze sprang up, and it was hard to keep our heavy boat bow on; but as the cries died down we could see dimly what seemed to be a raft with about 20 men standing on it, back to back. It was the overturned boat [collapsible B]; and as the sailors on our boat said we could still carry 8 or 10 more people, we called for another boat to volunteer and go to rescue them [lifeboat 12].

So we two cut loose our painters and between us got all the men off. They were nearly gone and could not have held out much longer. Then, when the sun rose we saw the *Carpathia* standing up about five miles away and for the first time saw the icebergs all around us.

The *Carpathia* steamed toward us until it was full daylight; then she stopped and began picking up boats, and we got on board about 8 o'clock. Very soon after we got on board they took a complete list

> of the names of all survivors. The kindness and the efficiency of all the arrangements on the *Carpathia* for our comfort can never be too highly praised.

Lifeboat 10 was launched by Chief Officer Wilde and Officer Murdoch at 1.50 am, from the portside at the rear of the ship. It was the last regular lifeboat to be launched.

It seems that Mark Fortune and his family had got to the boat deck near lifeboat 10. However, thinking that she was on a massive 'unsinkable' ship, Ethel decided that getting into a dingy lifeboat was a waste of time, and she left Alice and Mabel on deck to go back to the comfort of her cabin. Soon afterwards a steward informed her that her mother and sisters had got into a lifeboat. He escorted her to lifeboat 10, which was just being lowered, and she had to jump into the boat and the people had to catch her. Mark and young Charles went down with the ship and their bodies were never found.

A passenger named Clear Cameron noted: 'Officer Lowe decided to go back to search for survivors, and transferred all the passengers from lifeboat 14 into lifeboat 10. Lifeboat 14 was reportedly the only one which went back to look for survivors, and six victims were pulled from the water, but two of them died.' Two able seamen were transferred from lifeboat 10 into lifeboat 14, and Charles Williams was transferred from lifeboat 4.

Some people expressed a fear that they might be swamped by desperate people if they returned, so Lowe reluctantly agreed to wait until the screams from those in peril had died down a bit before he went back to help the desperate survivors. Lifeboat 14 made the journey of approximately 150 yards back to the disaster site, and when they arrived at the wreckage they were confronted with the dreadful sight of countless dead bodies floating in the icy water.

Seaman Joe Scarrott remembered:

> When we got to it the sight we saw was awful. We were amongst hundreds of dead bodies floating in lifebelts. We could only see

> four alive. The first one we picked up was a male passenger. He died shortly after we got him in the boat. After a hard struggle we managed to get the other three. One of these we saw kneeling as if in prayer upon what appeared to be a part of a staircase. He was only about twenty yards away from us but it took us half-an-hour to push our boat through the wreckage and bodies to get to him; even then we could not get very close, so we put out an oar for him to get hold of and so pulled him to the boat. All the bodies we saw seemed as if they had perished with the cold as their limbs were all cramped up. As we left that awful scene we gave way to tears. It was enough to break the stoutest heart.

During an interview with the *Sphere* periodical, Scarrott admitted: 'As we left that awful scene we gave way to tears.'

Willie Carter eventually got on board collapsible C, one of the last to leave the ship, having been launched from the starboard side by officers Wilde and Murdoch at 2 am. However, because lifeboat 4 had been attached to Officer Lowe's boats and had to wait until he got back from his rescue attempt, he arrived at the rescue ship before the rest of his family and waited on deck for lifeboat 4 to appear. He remembered that he did not recognise his son under the big lady's hat he was wearing and called out for him. Apparently, in response to second steward George Dodd's order that no more boys were to enter lifeboat 4, his mother had put the hat on his head, hoping that if he looked like a girl he should be allowed on the lifeboat – which he was.

Eventually, Bruce Ismay also got into collapsible C, and Mr Carter noted: 'Ismay and I and several officers walked up and down the deck of the sinking vessel for several minutes shouting, 'Any more women?' There was no response, and the officers then said that Ismay and I could enter the boat if we would consent to row. This we did until the *Carpathia* was sighted.'

Collapsible D was launched from the portside at about 2.05 am, from the same davits that had been used to launch emergency lifeboat 2, with officers Wilde and Lightoller taking charge of the procedure. As collapsibles A and B were washed off the boat deck soon after collapsible D, it was the last craft to be launched. Hugh Woolner and Frederick Hoyt ended up in this craft, which was eventually towed to *Carpathia* by Officer Lowe's lifeboat 14. There is a photograph of collapsible D being towed, which shows Hugh Woolner in a prominent position at the front.

Woolner remembered seeing what he described as 'a continent of ice'. He left a detailed account of his experiences, the transcripts of which are held at the Royal Museums in Greenwich:

> We were sitting, a party of about six, drinking hot whiskey and water. On Sunday night I noticed that everyone was drinking hot drinks. On the previous night iced drinks had been the favourites, but on Sunday night everyone seemed to be drinking grog. It had suddenly become deadly cold in the lounge and restaurant and the lady of our party had gone off to her room.
>
> Then we men strolled up just above the smoking room and had been seated only a few minutes when there came a heavy grinding shock beginning far ahead of us in the bows and rapidly passing along the ship and away under our feet. Everyone sprang up and ran through the swing doors astern. A man in front of me called out that he had seen an iceberg towering 50 feet above the deck, which was 100 feet above the sea, and passing away astern. This was the explanation.
>
> I went with a Swedish friend whose acquaintance I made on board, Bjornstroem-Steffansson of the Swedish Embassy in Washington. We sought out the lady who had been recommended to my care, Mrs Churchill Candee, who was returning from Paris to see her only son, who had met with a serious aeroplane accident in America. We found her and we took her up on to A deck to see how things were going.
>
> [Note: Mr Mauritz Bjornstroem-Steffansson's name was Anglicised to Maurice Stephenson, and both he and Helen Candee were members of the on-board 'Our Coterie', along with Hugh Woolner. Hugh and Helen may have been romantically involved].
>
> We found the engines stopped and the officers and crew making preparations to lower the boats. The officers were assuring everyone that there was no danger to life, but that the ladies were to be put into the boats as a precautionary measure. We continued our walk awhile, and then I saw passengers coming up with lifebelts on. I got Mrs Candee's tied on to her and then went off to my room and got on mine and brought away an extra one which I soon gave to some

scared person who had none. Bjornstroem and I took Mrs Candee up to the upper A deck where the boats were hung and we put her safely with a rug into the first boat, which gradually was filled with women and children, and a few of the crew were put in, three I think, and a youth with a broken arm. [This was lifeboat 6].

Not enough men were put into the first boats really. We then bade her a cheery goodbye and told her we should help her on board again when the ship had steadied herself. She wanted us to come too but we laughed this off.

We then went and helped with several more lifeboats, bundling in the women and children. Meanwhile several gentlemen were standing calmly by and looked on. Several men crept into these few boats, as it came out, and they give fatuous explanations how they came to do so. They were forced in by zealous friends against their own wish, and so on.

The calm courage of the passengers was most inspiring. Many women refused to leave without their husbands. Bjornstroem and I took many of them at their husbands' desire and bodily chucked them into the boats. Eventually all the lifeboats on the port side were launched, and while the crew were putting a big Berthon collapsible boat on the davits he and I went down to the lower deck and around to look for stray women.

We found three ladies close together and then we rushed them into a boat on the starboard side by sheer bluff. We shouted our way through the press, 'Make way for ladies!', and then we hoisted them up, one of us on each side, and giving them a final heave in they had to go, head over heels. We then turned our attention to a boat ready on the starboard side, where there was shouting going on.

We saw the first officer twice fire a pistol in the air ordering a crowd of crew out of the boat. We ran in and helped bundle the men out onto the deck and then we got a lot, about ten, Italian and other foreign women into that boat, and when we saw it was being safely lowered, we went away and made a final search on the deck below. The electric lights were beginning to turn red and not a soul was to be seen on the whole deck of 160 yards. The thick glass windows were all closed and Bjornstroem said to me, 'I think we may now make a try for ourselves'. I replied, 'All right!'

We walked along and through an open door beyond the glass windows, where there was an open gunwale. Looking out we saw the sea pouring over the bows and through the captain's bridge. Just opposite us was the collapsible boat [lifeboat D] which we had seen being hooked onto the last davits on the port side. She was being lowered into the sea and hung about nine feet away from us.

I said, 'Let's make a jump for it! There is plenty of room in her bows!' Bjornstroem replied, 'Right you are.'

We skipped on the gunwale, balanced ourselves for a moment and leaped into the air. He landed fair and square into the boat. I landed on my chest and caught hold with my hands on the gunwale and slipped off backwards. I hauled myself up with my arms and got my right foot over the gunwale. Bjornstroem said, 'All right, I've got you,' and levered me up by my right. But that time by left leg was in the sea, so it was a near thing.

Once in the lifeboat, Woolner continued:

We continued our course, for it would have been sheer madness to have returned and tried to pick up any more. It would have meant all of us perishing. The sea was as smooth as a pond or none of us would have been alive. The Titanic struck at 11.45 pm, on a starry, clear night. She finally sank at 2.22 am. I believe seventeen boats got away. I was in the seventeenth. The only thing I saved was my money. I worked all through the excitement with Bjornstroem at my side. We spoke with strong authority and people simply stood aside and made way for us when we came up with women in tow. It was remarkable! There were scenes of magnificent unselfishness and devotion: women who absolutely refused to go without their husbands; dozens of husbands who simply obeyed orders and remained silent and quiet on deck while their wives were put into safety. In particular a very handsome old gentleman, Mr Isidor Straus, and his wife were there and declined to be separated, and when we suggested that so old a man was justified in going into the boat that was waiting, Mr Straus said, 'Not before the other men.' His wife tightened her grasp on his arm and patted it and smiled up at him and then smiled at us.

In our boat we floated around for a long time in the dark, the cries getting fainter and fewer in the distance. Then a boat with an officer came along [Fifth Officer Harold Lowe with lifeboat 14] and he gave us orders for us all to form a string by making fast out painter's head and tail, so as to make a more conspicuous mark in the ocean for a passing ship to see. This we did and it gave us something to do.

After a while orders were given to lighten the officer's boat, so he could go and help some poor wretches on an upturned boat, which by now was faintly visible in the distance. We got seven more into our already pretty full boat, but we could stand them upright. Other boats got others, and the officer went away with his sail up and got in about twenty shivering men who had been balancing themselves for over three hours up to their ankles on an upturned collapsible boat. Think of it! Faint streaks of light began in the east by this time and I saw a breeze coming towards us, which was a serious matter in our heavily-loaded condition. I advised throwing off the painter and keeping her head into the sea. This was done. The wind continued to freshen.

Looking around, I saw about twenty icebergs that looked like photographs of the Antarctic expedition. The whole horizon was snow – the edge of a floe, which turned out to be about 40 miles long, and yet our lookout on the *Titanic* had seen nothing and we had been going full speed ahead all through the night. Then I saw a rocket, and a little later the lights of a steamer coming our way. This cheered us mightily, as you may imagine. Very slowly she seemed to come on, picking her way through the ice. Eventually she slowed down and then stopped and we saw boats about her sides and I understood that our first boat loads were being taken aboard.

The officer in the sail boat bore down on us, and seeing we were being rather roughly knocked about by the sea, gave us a tow, but started away from the steamer, and we then saw he was making for another set of unfortunates, who were standing up, apparently, in the water. They were a party of fourteen or so, among them a black-haired woman and two corpses.

The living having been taken aboard, we wore around and made for the ship, the breeze freshening all the while. It seemed a very long time, but eventually we came alongside the *Carpathia* on her way with a crowd of tourists on their way to Gibraltar. Getting under the lee side, we made fast, and soon had the women hoisted in a sling, and then we men clambered stiffly up the rope ladders.

Stewards steered us to the dining saloon, where hot brandy and water and biscuits awaited us. Seven hundred about were saved out of, I believe 2,500. Everything possible had been done on board to make us comfortable, and nothing could exceed the kindness the passengers on the *Carpathia* showed to the shivering people who came up out of the sea. I was given a sofa in the first officer's cabin. We had fogs nearly all the time since we were rescued and our speed was therefore moderate.

This general description will serve to show that the behaviour of the American and English passengers and of the whole crew was admirable, with very few exceptions.

After being told it would be best for them to get up onto the boat deck, Frederick Hoyt suggested that he and his wife should get warmly clad. He also stated that he looked out from the ship and saw *Titanic's* lights reflecting on a large iceberg. He escorted his wife to a lifeboat and saw her safely aboard, but just before the craft was lowered, Mrs Hoyt saw that her husband was still on the deck and she scrambled back out again. The next minute she was picked up by a member of the crew and forced into collapsible D. Frederick watched the craft being lowered and rowed away from the side of the ship. As he considered himself to be a good swimmer, and using his skills as a navigator on his yachts, he decided to dive overboard and swim in the direction he thought the boat would go. He did so, and after using a piece of wreckage as buoyancy, he found that his calculations were correct and he was only person to be picked up by collapsible D, the last boat to be rowed away from the ship. Mrs Hoyt was not aware that her husband was in the boat until they reached *Carpathia*, which was at about 7.15 am.

At 2.10 am, after collapsible C had been launched on the starboard side of the ship, officers Wilde, Murdoch and Moody, attempted to attach collapsible A to the same davit. Unfortunately, time had run out, as the ship was going down fast. The sea water began to engulf the deck and the lifeboat was washed over the side before the canvas sides had been put up. It became awash with water after the supports for its canvas sides were broken from the fall. Air tanks built into the craft prevented it from sinking entirely, and as their last desperate chance several people climbed on to it, but their weight turned it over and they were thrown back into the water. However, some did manage to climb back on board.

At about the same time as collapsible A was being launched, Officer Lightoller attempted to launch collapsible B. By this time the water had risen almost as high as the boat deck, as Officer Lightoller climbed on to the top of the officer's quarters, stripped the covers off collapsible B and cut away the ropes with a penknife. He was able to send the craft down to the flooded deck, but it flipped over.

Duane and Richard Norris Williams left their first-class stateroom on C Deck intending to go to the bar for drinks, but on the way they came across a steward who was trying to open a stuck door, which had passengers panicking in the room on the other side. In an attempt to help the situation, Richard rammed his shoulder against the door and broke in. The occupants were thankful, but the steward went into a huff and warned that he would report him to the White Star Line for damaging their property. To top it all, when they got to the bar another steward told them that it was closed, so they went to the gymnasium instead.

When they realised that the situation was serious, Duane and Richard went up to the boat deck, where they found that only the collapsible boats were left, and they had to dive for their lives. Unfortunately, when one of the funnels collapsed and crashed into the sea, Richard lost sight of his father.

The *Washington Times* for 22 April 1912, reported:

> Philadelphia gives up all hope of life of parent – Richard Norris Williams, junior, one of the survivors of the *Titanic*, who was coming to this city with his father after having spent many years abroad, is one of the few survivors who must absolutely give up all hope of life for his parent. Williams saw his father crushed to death by one of the enormous smoke stacks of the sinking vessel.
>
> 'We stood on the deck watching the lifeboats of the *Titanic* being filled and lowered into the water,' said Williams, 'the water was almost up to our waists and the ship was about at her last. Suddenly one of the great funnels fell. I sprang, endeavouring to pull my father with me. The funnel was swept overboard and my father's body went with it.
>
> 'I sprang overboard and swam through the ice to a life raft. I was pulled aboard. There were five men and one woman on the raft. Occasionally we were swept off into the sea, but always managed to crawl back. Finally, the Carpathia picked us up.'
>
> He later stated: 'I was not underwater very long, and as soon as I came to the top I threw off my big fur coat. About twenty yards away I saw something floating. I swam to it and found it to be a collapsible boat [A].' He also took off his shoes, which may have been a bad mistake as the bone-chilling water posed a serious threat to his limbs.
>
> There may have been about 30 people balancing or clinging to the flat boat as it drifted away from the disaster area, all shivering

with cold and up to their knees in cold water, and one by one they succumbed to the stress and cold. After awful suffering while floating precariously for several hours, Richard and about ten other survivors were eventually transferred to lifeboat D, which was then attached to lifeboat 14 and towed to *Carpathia*. The collapsible A craft was abandoned and left floating on the water.

When he was taken on board the rescue ship the doctor examined his leg and fearing hypothermia, so he advised amputation. However, Charles refused, 'I am going to need these legs,' he insisted. As he tried to stand up he remembered, 'It was like thousands of needles.' However, determined to restore feelings in his legs he walked the deck of the ship at regular intervals, and continued to do so when he returned to dry land.

LOST AT SEA

Thomas Andrews

Tommie Andrews was in his cabin working and was unaware of any problem until Captain Smith asked him to go up on the bridge as soon as possible. Sometime later he and Captain Smith were seen inspecting the front part of the ship, where they visited the flooded mail room and the squash court, which was quickly filling with water. When they got back to the bridge Mr Andrews informed the captain that he did not expect *Titanic* to stay afloat for more than two hours.

During that period, he spent his time walking about the decks encouraging passengers to wear their lifebelts. He was reportedly last seen without his own lifebelt, staring blankly at a painting above the mantel in the first-class smoking room.

Quigg Baxter

Just before midnight, Helene Baxter became concerned when she noticed that the ship had stopped, so she sent her son Quigg to investigate. He saw Captain Smith and Bruce Ismay in the corridor, and although Smith tried to reassure him before he rushed off, Mr Ismay advised him to get his mother and sister up to the boat deck. He carried his mother up the grand staircase and led his sister and his girlfriend Bertha to lifeboat 6.

As he placed them in the vessel he handed his mother a sterling silver flask of brandy, to which she complained about him drinking. He replied in French, 'Are you okay, Mum? Goodbye, and keep your spirits up everyone.' His sister remembered, 'Quigg didn't seem at all disturbed. While he didn't relish being parted from us, he bade me farewell bravely.' Bertha did not want to get into the boat without him, but the woman who came to be known as 'Unsinkable' Molly Brown persuaded her to do so. Quigg waved them away, and they never saw him again. His body was never identified.

Dai Bowen and Leslie Williams

Nothing is known about them after the collision, but both boxers lost their lives in the sinking, and the body of Leslie Williams was the fourteenth recovered by the *Mackay-Bennett*, and was buried at sea; his effects being returned to his family.

Thornton Davidson

When disaster struck, Thornton Davidson and his whole party made their way up to the boat deck. He and Mr Hays made sure the females got into lifeboat 3, and then they moved away, making no attempt to enter any of the lifeboats.

Mark and Charles Fortune

Apparently, Mark never went anywhere without wearing a heavy Winnipeg buffalo fur coat. His wife tried to discourage him from packing what she considered to be a useless moth-eaten garment, but Mark was insistent. He was wearing it when he arrived at the boat deck and joked how it had come in handy on such a cold night.

Thomas McCawley

During the evacuation Thomas remained in the gymnasium where he is said to have encouraged the passengers who found their way into the gym to try out the apparatus; possibly to take their minds off what was happening. He told a survivor that he would not put on a lifebelt because it would only hinder him as he made an attempt to swim for his life. His body was never recovered.

Clarence Moore

On the night of the disaster, Clarence had been playing cards in the smoking room with some of his dining companions, including Willie Carter, where he had told stories of his adventures in the mountains and forests of West Virginia, and of the time he had helped a newspaper reporter to gain an interview with the West Virginian Confederate outlaw, Captain William 'Devil Anse' Hatfield.

It is thought that Clarence and Major Butt, who was also from Washington, remained together until jumping into the icy waters of the Atlantic as the ship went down. Their bodies were never recovered.

Washington Roebling

After the collision Washington Roebling alerted Edith and Margaret Graham to the danger, and with the help of a friend they escorted them to lifeboat 3, one of the first to be launched on the starboard side of the ship, making no attempt to get in. Washington also helped Caroline Bonnell and Mary Wick into lifeboat 8, reassuring them, 'You will be back on board soon.' His body was never found.

Arthur Ryerson

On the night of the disaster, Arthur had been playing cards in the smoking room with some of his dining companions, including Willie Carter. According to Colonel Gracie, at 2 am, only twenty minutes before *Titanic* sank, he, along with Major Archibald Butt, the painter Frank Millet and Clarence Moore, returned to their usual table in the first-class smoking lounge to play a final game of cards, before shaking hands and departing.

Peter Sloan

Peter Sloan was one of ten electricians on board the ship, who were known to have kept the lights on for as long as they could so that passengers could see their way to the lifeboats; after which they all lost their lives. Peter body was not recovered.

James Clinch Smith

During the course of the voyage, seven individuals on board had formed what they referred to as 'Our Coterie'. This was based on a famous fashionable set of English aristocrats and intellectuals of the Edwardian period, known as 'The Coterie'. Colonel Archibald Gracie seems to have instigated the exclusive group, and James Smith and Hugh Woolner were members.

A party of three woman and a man, along with a Pomeranian dog, were standing on the boat deck waiting to board lifeboat 7, the first to leave the ship, when James Smith, who had 'showed no sign of fear' walked by and jokingly commented, 'Oh, I suppose we ought to put a life preserver on the little doggie, too.'

He was an old friend of Colonel Gracie. They were table companions, and Colonel Gracie stated that they were together from the beginning to the end of the voyage. The colonel stated in his book:

> On the night of the terrible disaster when I came up on the deck after having been aroused from my slumbers, I met Smith, and we made an agreement to stick to each other through thick and thin. We first realized the gravity of the situation while we were still on a lower deck when we noticed the list the ship gave toward the port side. We took up our station on the port side of the boat deck, at the bow end, near where women and children were being loaded into one of the boats. Here, without any seeming fear whatsoever, Smith stood and he and I helped lift women and children and babies over the rail as each boat was loaded and then lowered.
>
> Toward the last, when the list of the vessel became such that Second Officer Lightoller ordered all passengers to the starboard side, Smith at once obeyed and I followed. Here he calmly took in all that was being done by the crew in an attempt to launch a collapsible canvas

boat that had been slid down from the hurricane deck, and he and I helped. Before the boat could be launched, the water was upon us.

When Smith and I saw that there was little chance of getting the boat and that it would be overcrowded, when we heard and saw the water rise to the boat deck, we decided to move toward the stern. Still on the starboard side, our progress was blocked by a mass of humanity, which suddenly appeared from the decks below and consisted of second class or steerage passengers.

Behind us the water approached rapidly, and we entered a cull de sac to which the only outlet was the bridge deck above. Smith tried to reach it by jumping and so did I, but the height was too great for us. The water was now upon us and just as it struck, I rose with a jump at the same time, and was carried high up, when I grasped the brass railing around the bridge deck and held on with might and main. Then I looked hastily to the right and left, but Smith was gone. I never saw him again. Undoubtedly he was engulfed by the waters and went down with the ship.

Words fail to express the feelings of admiration which I have for his conduct, and the highest tribute I could pay him is this plain recital of what he did in the way of self-sacrifice, knowing no such word as fear in saving the lives of others. His relatives and friends should be proud of him and his record in this terrible disaster.

John Thayer

During all the confusion, John Thayer became separated from his son Jack, but he managed to get his wife Marian and Margaret, his maid, to lifeboat 4. Marian and Margaret got into lifeboat 4 and it would seem that John stepped back to await his fate. He seems to have stayed with his travelling companions, the Wideners and Duane Williams. When all the lifeboats had been launched, Colonel Gracie stated that he saw Mr Thayer at the starboard front of the ship, 'looking pale and determined'. When he returned a short time later, John Thayer was nowhere to be seen. His body, if recovered, was never identified.

Duane Williams

At 6.38 pm on Sunday, 14 April, Duane Williams sent a message to his brother in Philadelphia, stating, 'Arrive Wednesday Titanic. Send Marconigram how you are. Fine voyage.'

Frederick Wright

Colonel Archibald Gracie had decided that he had neglected his health recently and wanted to spend some time doing physical exercise on the squash courts and in the swimming pool, so he booked in with Fred Wright, the squash court attendant on Sunday, 14 April, and booked another session for 7.30 am on the Monday.

After the collision Colonel Gracie met Fred, who looked quite worried. Probably to reassure the 24-year-old, the colonel said jokingly, 'Hadn't we better cancel that appointment?' The reason for Fred's worried look was because he knew that the squash court and his cabin were flooded, and so he simply replied, 'Yes, we better.' Fred Wright could not swim. His body was never recovered. Colonel Gracie escaped from the ship clinging to Collapsible B.

* * *

An at-a-glance list and approximate time schedule concerning the launching of the lifeboats:

Time	*place*	*number*	*Relevant escapees*
00.40	starboard for	lifeboat 7	
00.45	starboard for	lifeboat 5	Karl Behr and Mrs Stengel
00.55	starboard for	lifeboat 3	Harry Anderson and Thornton Davidson's party
00.55	portside for	lifeboat 4	(not successfully)
01.00	portside for	lifeboat 8	Mr Roebling escorted women to this boat
01.05	starboard for	lifeboat E1	Sir Cosmo and wife; Charles Stengel
01.10	portside for	lifeboat 6	Major Arthur Peuchen and the Baxter family
01.20	portside aft	lifeboat 16	Charles Andrews

01.25	portside aft	lifeboat 14	R Norris Williams (after lifeboats CA and CD)
01.30	portside aft	lifeboat 12	Jack Thayer transferred from lifeboat CB
01.30	starboard aft	lifeboat 9	James Widgery
01.35	starboard aft	lifeboat 11	
01.40	starboard aft	lifeboat 13	
01.40	starboard aft	lifeboat 15	Fred Dymond
01.45	portside for	lifeboat E2	
01.50	portside for	lifeboat 4	Ryerson family; Charles Williams, Mrs Thayer
01.50	portside aft	lifeboat 10	Fortune family
02.00	starboard	lifeboat CC	Bruce Ismay and Willie Carter
02.05	portside	lifeboat CD	Hugh Woolner
02.10	starboard	lifeboat CA	R. Norris Williams (then lifeboats CD and 14)
02.10	portside	lifeboat CB	Jack Thayer

for forward (front)

aft (rear)

E emergency

C collapsible

THEIR HEARTS WILL GO ON

Concise Biographical Tributes

Henry 'Harry' Anderson
Sailing

Harry Anderson was born in Manhattan, New York, on 20 October 1869, the son of Henry Rhind Anderson (1833-1911), originally of South Leith in Midlothian, Scotland, a gold broker who had moved to the United States in 1851, and his New Yorker wife Elizabeth Antoinette (formerly Draper, 1841-1895). He had an older brother named Charles and an older sister named Elizabeth (Bessie). His father had returned to the UK in 1891.

In 1902 he became a member of the yacht division of the New York Athletic Club, being appointed a commodore, and later became a member of the Larchmont Yacht Club in New York.

At the Church of Transfiguration in New York on 8 April 1907, he married Grace Irene Ryder (1876-1915). They lived on the upper west side of Manhattan at 823 West End Avenue.

Harry spent the summer of 1911 with his father, whose address was at Regent Street in Middlesex, until he died on 1 August of that year. He sailed back to New York on the *Minnehaha* in the following month, but was back in London in March 1912 for business and pleasure.

When he was on board the rescue ship he tried to send a telegram to his wife, which read, 'Safe aboard *Carpathia*. Do not worry,' but due to the volume of requests the wireless operator did not transmit it. The message was sold at auction in 2011. His dog is thought to have died in the sinking. He left no known account of his experiences on *Titanic.*

Grace died at the age of 38, in Manhattan on 9 June 1915. On 24 August 1926, Harry married a widow named Florence 'Flora' Gardner (formerly Mackley). Flora died on 7 December 1937, aged 55.

Harry continued to travel to London at various times, and his 1919 passport described him as being 5 feet 5 inches tall, with a fair complexion, grey hair and grey eyes. At that time he lived at 203 West 103rd Street, and worked at Roderick and Rumsey at 10 Bridge Street in New York City.

Harry lived the last twenty years of his life at Pelham Manor, situated at 950 Grant Avenue in New York. Like Frederick Hoyt, he died in at the New Rochelle Hospital in New York, on 23 November 1951, aged 82, and was buried with Flora in the Mackley family mausoleum at Woodlawn Cemetery in the Bronx district of New York.

Charles Edward Andrews
Swimming

Charles Andrews was born at West Derby in Liverpool, on 18 January 1893, the third of five sons in the family of eight children born between 1881 and 1898, to Henry Jeremiah Andrews (1857-1919), and his wife, Emily Anne (formerly Robertson, 1859-1920), who had married in their native town of Southampton in 1879. Henry was a seaman, and it was his work which took him north to Liverpool.

The 1891 census records his family living at a house called 'Oakleigh' on Bedford Road in the district of Walton-on-the-Hill in Liverpool, but two decades later they had moved back south to 145 Millbrook Road in the district of Freemantle, Southampton. Charles reportedly went to sea at the age of 15 so therefore was absent from the 1911 census.

Charles was on board *Olympic* when it collided with *Hawke*, and had been with the White Star Line for four years, having previously served on RMS *Oceanic*. He was aged 19 when he signed-on to *Titanic* as an assistant officer's saloon steward, on 10 April 1912. His cousin, George Robertson, also signed on as a steward. His address when he signed on *Titanic* was 125 Millbrook Road in Southampton. He was called to give evidence at the United States Senate Inquiry on Day 7, 25 April 1912.

He signed on to *Oceanic* again on 10 July 1912. He served on RMS *Aquitania* as a steward, sailing in both world wars, the only true ocean liner to do so. Launched right before the onset of the First World War, the *Aquitania* did not see much civilian service before being requisitioned for the war effort. She was set to be re-equipped to sail as an armed merchant cruiser, but when it was decided that the transition would be too expensive, she was kitted out as a troopship and carried soldiers to the different battle fronts around the world. When it was decided that hospital ships were needed, *Aquitania* joined RMS *Britannic* in transporting wounded soldiers.

Before the Second World War she had been set to retire, but the British Admiralty decided to utilise her as a troop transport, sailing mostly between Britain and Canada. She survived the war and continued to sail, making her the longest serving Cunarder until 2004, when the *Queen Elizabeth II* surpassed the record.

In 1932 Charles married Ivy Winifred Powell at Millbrook Church in Southampton. She had been born on 1 January 1903, at Eling in Totton, Hampshire. They had children named Ann Marina, born in 1934; and Edward, born in 1937. Charles served on the *Queen Mary* as a masseur and swimming pool attendant, and then on the *Queen Elizabeth* until his retirement in 1959.

Charles died in Southampton on 2 January 1961, aged 67. He was cremated and his ashes were scattered at the South Stoneham Cemetery in Swaythling, Southampton. His wife died in 1976.

Thomas Andrews
Cricket

Thomas Andrews, who became known as Tommie, was born into a prominent administrative Ulster family on 7 February 1873, at Ardara House in Comber near Newtownards, County Down, Ireland. The house is now divided into flats, including a Titanic Suite. Tommie was the second son of the Right Honourable Thomas Andrews (1843-1916), a member of the Privy Council of Ireland, and his wife, Eliza (formerly Pirrie, 1845-1929). His older brother was John Miller Andrews, who was Prime Minister of Northern Ireland from 1940 to 1943, and his younger brother was Sir James Andrews, who was Lord Chief Justice of Northern Ireland from 1937 to 1951. He was a nephew of Lord William James Pirrie, the principal owner of the Harland and Wolff Company in Belfast.

He has been described as: 'A healthy, energetic, bonny child, who grew into a handsome, plucky and lovable boy.' Like his father and other members of the family, he was educated at the Royal Belfast Academical Institution from 1884, and in 1889, aged just 16, he gained employment at the Harland and Wolff Shipyard as an apprentice. He was under the guidance of his uncle, however it is recorded that he showed great aptitude and industry, and during this time he studied in the evenings.

Tommie was a keen cricketer, and all the men in his family played for the North Down Cricket Club at Comber in Northern Ireland. They even donated the ground that is still used by the club to this day, and a trophy for the player of the year. He organised a game between North Down CC and Harland and Wolff CC, and chose to play for his work's team, but the North Down bowlers got him out without scoring.

After the completion of his apprenticeship, his promotion was rapid and entirely due to his own ability and energy. He became very popular, and was appointed as one of the outside managers in the shipyard. In 1894 he was given charge of the repair department, in which capacity his abilities were thoroughly tested as some of the most difficult engineering achievements were supervised by him at a very young age. He was involved in the repair and construction of numerous vessels, including the *Baltic* and the *Oceanic*. He was noted as a hardworking man and for his innovative designs, and became the manager of the design department.

Among his memberships of several influential institutions, he became a member of the Royal Institution of Naval Architects in 1901, and the Institution of Mechanical Engineers in 1902.

In 1907 he was appointed a managing director at Harland and Wolff. In the same year the White Star Line decided to create a class of luxury liners and the project was given to Harland and Wolf. Consequently, Tommie became the main architect of both the *Olympic* and the *Titanic*.

On 24 June 1908 he married Helen Reilly Barbour (born at Warwick on 10 April 1881). She was the daughter of the textile industrialist, John Doherty Barbour. They made their home at a house called 'Dunallan' at 20 Windsor Avenue in Belfast. On 27 November 1910, they had a daughter named Elizabeth Law Barbour Andrews, who was usually known by her initials of ELBA. She became the first woman ever to receive a pilot's licence in Northern Ireland.

On Tommie's untimely death, the Institution of Mechanical Engineers stated: 'His knowledge of naval architecture embraced electrical and mechanical engineering as well as marine engineering, his experience of all the complicated and intricate machinery and arrangements necessary in the construction and equipment of modern steam ships being altogether exceptional.'

His wife received the following letter from Bruce Ismay:

> Forgive me for intruding upon your grief, but I feel I must send you a line to convey my most deep and sincere sympathy with you in the terrible loss you have suffered. It is impossible for me to express in words all I feel, or make you realise how truly sorry I am for you, or how my heart goes out to you. I knew your husband for many years, and had the highest regard for him, and looked upon him as a true

> friend. No one who had the pleasure of knowing him could fail to realise and appreciate his numerous good qualities and he will be sadly missed in his profession. Nobody did more for the White Star Line, or was more loyal to its interests than your good husband, and I always placed the utmost reliance on his judgment.
>
> If we miss him and feel his loss so keenly, what your feelings must be I cannot think. Words at such a time are useless, but I could not help writing to you to tell you how truly deeply I feel for you in your grief and sorrow.

On 8 February 1917, Helen married Henry Peirson Harland, a member of the family of the owners of the shipyard. She died in Northern Ireland on 22 August 1966, aged 85. His daughter Elizabeth never married and was killed in a traffic accident in County Dublin, Ireland on 1 November 1973. There are no living descendants of Thomas Andrews, but his wife had four children with her second husband and there are living descendants of that lineage.

The SS *Nomadic,* the only ship designed by Tommie that still survives, remains on display in Belfast in his honour. His name appears on the Titanic Memorial in the Memorial Gardens at Belfast City Hall. He was in his fortieth year at the time of his death, and in James Cameron's 1997 film *Titanic* he was portrayed by Victor Garber, a 48-year-old Canadian.

Quiggley Edmond 'Quigg' Baxter

Athletics / Track and Field, American Football and Ice Hockey

Quigg Baxter was born in Montreal, Canada, on 13 July 1887. He was the son of Irish-born James Baxter (1840-1905) and Helene de Lanaudiere Chaput (1881-1923), who was a descendant of French-Canadian aristocracy. They had married on 17 June 1882, at the Montreal Congregational Church. His father had built the Baxter Block in Montreal in 1892, which is considered to have been the first shopping mall in Canada. He became notorious as 'Diamond Jim' Baxter, who, as a diamond trader and banker, was convicted of fraud in 1900, and sentenced to five years in prison. He died soon after his release in 1905.

A son named Anthony William was born to the family in 1883, but he seems to have died as an infant, and Quigg had an older sister named Helene Jane (1885-1954), known as Suzette. Quigg was educated at the prestigious Loyola Jesuit College in Montreal and had enrolled in applied sciences at McGill University.

However, sport was his true passion, and he dropped out of school to pursue it. A member of the Montreal Amateur Athletic Association, as a teenager he earned a reputation as a star American football player and played ice hockey for the Montreal Shamrocks until 1907, when he was hit in the eye by a hockey stick and lost the sight in it. He then turned to coaching ice hockey, and is credited with organising the first ever ice hockey tournament in Paris. He soon returned to playing the game, and in 1912 played for Les Patineurs de Paris Hockey Club in an amateur hockey tournament at Chamonix in France, where they beat the Oxford Canadians.

As stated earlier, Quig had been coaching ice hockey in Switzerland and France, and had been joined by his mother and his sister. He had met a Belgian cabaret singer named Bertha Mayne, and had acquired cabin C-90 for her in the name of Mme DeVilliers, which was her stage name.

His name is commemorated on his mother's monument in Notre-Dame-des-Neiges Cemetery in Montreal.

Karl Howell Behr
Lawn Tennis and Ice Hockey

Karl Behr was born in Brooklyn, New York City, on 30 May 1885. He was a twin with his brother Paul (who may not have survived), and was a son of Herman Behr (1849-1934), the owner of Herman Behr and Company, and his wife Grace (formerly Howell, 1856-1907). His older brother was Max Behr, a well-known golfer, and there were nine children in all, including twin sisters born in 1886. Herman Behr was a successful abrasives manufacturer, and their home was the impressive Herman Behr Mansion, at 82 Pierrepoint Street, on the corner with Henry Street, at Brooklyn Heights in

New York, which was described as 'the city's finest Romanesque Revival' building.

He was educated at Lawrenceville School in New Jersey and attended Yale University's Sheffield Scientific School. He was admitted to the bar association in 1910. While at Yale he met Theodore Roosevelt and later worked as a booster for Roosevelt in the 1912 Progressive Party campaign, during which he organised some of the largest rallies in New York City.

He was in the baseball and American football teams, and played ice hockey for three years while at Yale. He was described by a newspaper as a 'golfing star', and was a member of the Crescent Athletic Club in Brooklyn.

However, it was at lawn tennis that Karl excelled. He was captain of the junior and senior tennis teams, and acted as vice-president for the Intercollegiate Tennis Association, 1904-1905, having won the intercollegiate doubles title in 1904. He played in the United States national championship all-comers final in 1906. In 1907 he reached the fourth round of the singles at Wimbledon, losing to the eventual champion Norman Brookes of Australia in five sets; and partnered by fellow-American Beals Wright, was runner-up in the doubles to Norman Brookes and Tony Wilding of New Zealand, in three sets. He reached number three in the United States' tennis rankings in the same year.

While returning to New York on *Carpathia,* he and several other survivors formed a committee to honour the bravery of Captain Rostron and his crew. They presented the captain with a silver cup and medals to each of the 320 crew members.

On 18 July 1912, at the venue of the Longwood Bowl Tournament played at the Longwood Cricket Club in Boston, Karl faced his fellow *Titanic* survivor Richard Norris Williams. After losing the first two sets, Karl won 0-6, 7-9, 6-2, 6-1, 6-4. However, Richard beat Karl in straight sets in the quarter-finals on his way to winning the

United States Open Tennis Championships at Newport, Rhode Island in 1914. They also met several times in doubles matches.

His sister Gertrude was friends with Helen Newsom, and she had caught Karl's eye. They married on 1 March 1913, at the Church of Transfiguration. They had three sons and a daughter: Karl Howell Junior in 1913, Peter in 1915, James in 1920 and Sally in 1928.

At the Sea Bright Tournament in New Jersey, held on 14 August 1915, Karl defeated Maurice McLoughlin, who was ranked number one in the world that year, to challenge Richard Norris Williams for the Achilles Cup, but he lost 6-7, 4-6, 6-3, 2-6. Consequently, the two *Titanic* survivors were chosen for the 1914 United States Davis Cup squad, but Karl did not play in the Challenge Round against Australasia at Forest Hills. Nevertheless, he reached number three in the United States' rankings for a second time that year.

The *Sydney Referee* for 22 September 1915, reported under the title 'McLoughlin Beaten by Behr: Maurice McLoughlin Beaten "At His Own Game" by Behr.':

> Maurice McLoughlin was defeated by Karl Behr in the final round of the Seabright Lawn Tennis and Cricket Club's invitation singles.
>
> Where the pick of the world's greatest players had failed in the Davis Cup matches Behr succeeded – and succeeded in a manner that was convincing. He beat the red-headed rapier at his own game – overwhelmed him by the sheer impetuosity of his attack, and did not allow him a single set. Behr won at 8-6, 7-5, 7-5, and with his win the right to meet Richard Norris Williams, Harvard 76, in the challenge round for the Achilles Cup.
>
> In the first set both players seemed to be extremely cautious. They pulled their strokes, but as the match progressed they threw caution to the wind. Behr especially was reckless, but it was this recklessness that actually accounted for his surprising play. McLoughlin could not get started. Nine times during this set service games were lost. This was an unusual occurrence, and indicated that they were playing unsteady tennis.
>
> In the second set, however, five service games were lost, and therefore the tennis was better. Mac improved in his driving, while Behr was more accurate in his smashing. Behr won the first three

> games of the third set, and then indulged in one of his erratic flights. Mac took advantage of this, steadied down, and took the next four. He also won the ninth, and that was the end. Behr took the next three.
>
> Richard Norris Williams, of Philadelphia, the national singles tennis champion, added another victory to his string by out-classing arid out-playing Karl Behr, the Middle States champion, over the courts of the Seabright Tennis and Cricket Club, three sets to one. The score was 7-4, 6-4, 3-6, 6-2.
>
> Behr failed to show the form he displayed against McLoughlin, and Williams was in no danger at any stage of the game. The victory gives Williams a second leg on the. Achilles Cup trophy.
>
> Williams was cool and collected throughout, while Behr stormed and ranted as he netted ball after ball. Secretary of War Garrison was among the crowd, which was the largest one of the week.
>
> Behr won the first three games during his furious attack, but he lost his precision, thereafter. The last set provided some thrillingly even play, as Williams alternated on the first four games, then pulled out of the set at 6-2, with 30 points to the other's 19.

The *Sydney Morning Herald* for 14 August 1916, reported: '"Sport in America" – Norris Williams of Philadelphia has won the tennis championships for the third year. Clarence Griffin and William Johnston, the national champions, defeated Karl Behr and Frederick Alexander in the doubles.'

He served in the First World War as captain in the Motor Transport Sports Corps, later becoming a member of the Association of ex-members of Squadron A.

Under the title 'Stars for Active Service' the *Sydney Referee* for 23 May 1917, reported:

> R. Norris Williams II, the national lawn tennis champion in the singles, George M. Church, Dean Mathey, Watson M. Washburn, and others of the top-ranking players are preparing to take active service for their country in the war against Germany. Karl H. Behr, the famous international player, is being specially coached for a commission, and there is evidence that the followers of the courts will be well represented in the Army and Navy.
>
> Whatever may be done as to playing or curtailing the tournament schedule, it is probable that few, if any of the ranking men will

> appear in competitions, this season. Williams is at Governor's Island undergoing active training to enter the artillery corps: There is the possibility that his division may be sent to a preparatory camp along the Mexican border within a month.

Karl went into banking as vice-president of Dillon, Read and Company, of New York; and he was also on the board of the Fisk and Runner Company; the Goodyear Tire and Rubber Company; and the National Cash Register Company.

The family address was 215E 72nd Street in New York City, and he was president of the Inter-chemical Corporation, the Behr Manning Corporation of Troy, New York, and the Witherbee Sherman Corporation. He was a member of the Downtown Club, the University of Yale Club, and the Saint Nicholas Society of the City of New York.

Karl died of cancer on 15 October 1949, aged 64, at Morristown in New Jersey, and was buried at the Evergreen Cemetery in Morristown.

Helen married Dean Mathey, who was one of Karl's tennis friends, and she died in 1965.

In 1969 Karl was inducted into the International Tennis Hall of Fame at the Newport Casino Complex on Rhode Island.

In a book which was published at the time of the centenary, it was stated that Karl Behr was instrumental in persuading the *Carpathia*'s doctor not to amputate Richard Williams' damaged limbs; and when Williams defeated Karl Behr in the quarter-finals of the United States Open on his way to the title, Behr says to Williams, 'I should have let them cut off your legs.' These two incidents did not happen and were made up for dramatic effect and commercial purposes. Karl Behr's grand-daughter was not impressed by the way Karl had been depicted in the book, and she wrote a version of her own.

David John 'Dai' Bowen

Boxing

David Bowen, known as Dai, was born on 30 July 1891, at 42 Raglan Street in Ystradyfodwg near Treherbert in south Wales. He was the second son of three in the family of eight children, born between 1876 and 1894, to James Bowen of Merthyr Tydfil, and his wife Leah (formerly Protheroe, 1855-1918). They had married in 1873. The 1891 census records the family as living at 35 Bagnall Street in Treherbert. A decade later they had moved to the house next door and James Bowen had died. Dai's Uncle John (Protheroe) was the publican at the nearby *Royal Oak Hotel*, and Leah remarried in 1902, to become Mrs Morris Owen. At the time of the 1911 census the family lived at 42 Bagnall Street, and Dai was described as an unmarried coal miner, hewer.

At that time the Welsh valleys were producing good boxers such as Jim Driscoll and Jimmy Wilde of Cardiff, and Dai turned his hand to boxing. He was trained by a former British Army physical instructor named George Cundick, who also trained Leslie Williams. His fight record was as follows (*denotes the bout was not fully recognised):

2 April 1910 – beat Young Roberts at Millfield Air Corps in Pontypridd

20 August 1910 – drew with Jack Till at Pentre

10 April 1911 – lost to Young Johnny Walters at Millfield Air Corps in Pontypridd

14 October 1911 – beat Gus Venn at Millfield Air Corps in Pontypridd

*11 November 1911 – Batt McCarthy at Olympia Rink in Hartlepool

20 November 1911 – lost to Jerry Delaney at South Shields

25 November 1911 – beat Billy Grant at Olympia Rink in Hartlepool

*5 March 1912 – Young Johnny Walters at the Park Hall in Cardiff

The bout on 5 March was part of a charity tournament held by Nazareth House, a Roman Catholic institution. Leslie Williams also took part.

Local Press recorded:

> Mr Torreyson, a well-known Pittsburg racing man, wrote to a Cardiff newspaper reporter named Charles A Barnett, offering to defray the expenses of two good Welsh boxers. Many applications were received, and, although they were not the first choices, Dai Bowen and Leslie Williams were selected as men likely to meet with success. Bowen was a featherweight of considerable promise. In the contests he had fought in he showed signs of developing into a splendid man. Williams, a bantamweight, was the more experienced boxer.

The scheduled fights included one against the legendary Chicago boxer, Packey McFarland, who had only lost one of nearly one hundred fights.

After the *Titanic* disaster it was recorded by Charles Barnett:

> It seems but a moment ago since the two young boxers gripped my hand in farewell from the train which took them to Southampton. What strange fate! They were definitely fixed-up to sail by the *Lusitania* four days earlier, but poor Leslie Williams called on me to say that he wanted to wait for some suits of clothes to be made, as things were rather dear in America.
>
> 'Very well!' I said, 'we will go to the shipping agent and see what other boats are going, and I will send another cable to say that you are not going by the *Lusitania*.'
>
> We immediately went to the agent's office, and when Leslie heard that the world's largest liner was going to make a maiden trip on the following Wednesday he was simply delighted.
>
> 'That will give me a few days over the holidays.' He remarked to the manager of the office, and then left for home.

They could consider themselves to be very fortunate indeed. Three other boxers had been chosen to go to the States at first, but because of other commitments they could not make the trip, so Dai and Leslie were asked to go instead. A newspaper reported:

> Fred Dyer was next approached, and would have accepted, for, as he stated: 'his luck had been so bad over here in the way of accidents and interruptions to matches which had been arranged that he felt it could not be any worse in America and might be better. But just

> before going down to Nazareth House he saw another specialist about his knee, and was strongly advised to rest it absolutely for the next three months.'

Still known to his mother as David John and not Dai, he had written a letter to her and posted it in Queenstown:

> I am just writing you a few lines before I go sick, for I have been very good so far. This is a lovely boat, she is very near as big as Treherbert, she is like a floating palace, against you walk from one end of her to the other you are tired. We are landing in France at the time I am writing you this, you don't know whether she is moving or not for she goes very steady.
>
> Dear Mother, I hope that you won't worry yourself about me. I can tell you that I am a lot better than I thought I would be, for we get plenty of fun on board. We met two Swansea boys at the station, so you see that I get plenty of company. There are hundreds of foreigners on her of every nation. The food we get here is very good but not as good as dear old home. We have no boxing gloves with us; they would be no good if we did have some. Remember me to Martha Jane and Jack and Tommy Ostler. Tell Morris and Stephen that if I will feel like I do now when I land in Yankee Land I shall be alright. I shan't give you an address now, not until I land for it won't be worth it. I did not see David Rees in Southampton at all.
>
> Remember me to all I know, tell Stephen to tell all the boys that I am enjoying myself alright so far. If James tells you that I have not wrote to him, tell him that I can't do it very good now, you can show him this if you like, for it will be the same I shall have to say now for the time being as I am telling you. I hope you will excuse the pencil for I have no pen and ink, so cheer up now mother, for I am in the pink, so don't vex. I think I will draw to a close now in wishing you all my best love.

Dai and Leslie Williams booked their passage through the Dean and Dawson Tourist and Steamship Company in Cardiff, and paid extra for the third-class tickets so that they could have use of the first-class gymnasium to keep themselves in shape during the voyage.

Dai's family wrote several newspaper tributes to him until the Second World War, and paid for a grave site memorial dedicated to

The last known photograph of *Titanic* as it left southern Ireland on its doomed voyage across the North Atlantic Ocean.

Harry Anderson was a Wall Street stockbroker. A keen sailor, like Frederick Hoyt, he was a commodore of the New York Yacht Club and later the Larchmont Yacht Club of New York. An untransmitted telegram he wrote to his wife was auctioned in 2011.

Charles Andrews, from Liverpool, signed on *Titanic* as a second-class saloon steward. He was known to have gained awards for his swimming abilities.

Thomas Andrews was the chief designer of RMS *Titanic* at Harland and Wolff. He was a keen cricketer, and all the men in his family played the game. He lost his life in the disaster.

Quigg Baxter was a member of the Montreal Amateur Athletic Association. As a teenager he earned a reputation as a star American football player and played ice hockey for the Montreal Shamrocks until he was seriously injured. He then took up coaching the game. He lost his life in the sinking.

Karl Behr had played on the United States Davis Cup team of 1907, and was the Wimbledon doubles runner-up in the same year. He was on *Titanic* in pursuit of a girl. He is said to have proposed to her in a lifeboat, and married her in the following year.

Dai Bowen was considered to have a successful career in boxing ahead of him. He had recently got married and was on his way to the United States with Leslie Williams to take part in a championship, when he lost his life in the sinking.

A good horseman and a keen polo player, William Carter was travelling with his socialite wife, Lucile, their two daughters and a nephew. They had been staying in Leicestershire, where he had managed a few games of his favourite sport and had also found time to go hunting with the local foxhounds. He took his car, two polo ponies and two dogs with him when he boarded *Titanic*.

Lucile Stewart Carter was the daring socialite wife of William Carter. She was the first woman to ride astride a polo pony instead of side-saddle and could handle a coach-and-four with great skill.

Thornton Davidson was the son of a Canadian lawyer and judge. Like several of his siblings he was an accomplished sportsman at sailing, ice hockey, lawn tennis and equestrianism. He lost his life in the disaster.

Sir Cosmo Duff-Gordon (second from left) was a landowner and sportsman. A member of the International Olympic Committee, he had gained an Olympic fencing silver medal at what was known as the Interim Games held in Athens in 1906, to celebrate the tenth anniversary of the first Games held in that city in 1896. He was also a wrestler who took part in the mixed martial art known as Bartitsu, which was immortalised in the Sherlock Holmes books. A marble bust of him was sold at auction in 2020.

Frank Dymond (right) was said to be a hard man, who took part in boxing matches on board ships. He also fought in the professional ring and trained and seconded other young boxers.

Mark Fortune, a Canadian real-estate agent, was a keen curler and president of the Granite Curling Club in Winnipeg. He lost his life in the disaster.

Charles Fortune graduated from college with citations for academic and athletic excellence, particularly in ice hockey. Along with his father, he lost his life in the sinking.

Frederick Hoyt was an American broker, and, like Harry Anderson, was a noted member of the New York Yacht Club. He owned several prestigious yachts and took part in international races.

J. Bruce Ismay was chairman and managing director of the White Star Line. He had been a talented tennis player in his younger days, having won the Waterloo Championships in Liverpool, and the Northern Mixed Doubles Championships at Manchester in 1883, which was later moved to the All England Club at Wimbledon.

Thomas McCawley was the gymnasium steward with the victualling crew, who had embarked at Belfast for the delivery trip to Southampton. A former miner and ex-army man, he lost his life in the sinking.

Clarence Moore was known as one of the finest horsemen in Washington DC. He was also a good sailor, being a member of the Chevy Chase Equestrian Club, and, like Harry Anderson and Frederick Hoyt, was a member of the New York Yacht Club. He had been in England to acquire foxhounds for the Loudon Hunt in Virginia, of which he was hunt master. He lost his life in the sinking.

Major Arthur Peuchen owned a yacht that crossed the Atlantic Ocean under its own canvas and was commodore of the Royal Canadian Yacht Club. He offered his services as an experienced sailor to row a lifeboat and climbed down a rope to get to it.

Washington Roebling had been a promising American Football player in his youth, but his fascination with motor cars prompted him to join the pioneers of the early days of motor sport. He co-designed and built his own car, the Roebling-Planche Racer, and was returning from a motoring tour of Europe. He lost his life in the disaster.

Arthur Ryerson was the owner of the Otsego Golf Club at Cooperstown, New York, from 1901 until his death, and was one of the two western delegates who went to New York in 1895 to assist in forming the United States Golf Association. He lost his life in the sinking.

Jack Ryerson was refused a place in a lifeboat until his father intervened. He was a promising young golfer, who went on to compete in over 400 tournaments around the world.

Peter Sloan was the chief electrician on *Titanic*. He was a member of the Valkyrie Football Club in Liverpool, and during his employment with a number of the White Star ships he won the half-mile championship for swimming during the Italy versus England gala at Spezia, and a gold medal and silver cup. He lost his life in the sinking.

James Clinch Smith was a member of most of New York's elite clubs. He was a skilful yachtsman, and a multi-prize-winning rider at the New York Horse Show. He had actually built his own racing track at Smithtown. He lost his life in the sinking.

Charles Henry Stengel was described on his passport as having blue eyes and brown hair. He had a round face and chin, a high forehead and a regular nose. He was a Newark leather manmufacturer, who also owned several racehorses; and almost became the victim of a racing scam perpetrated by a dodgy fellow passenger on *Titanic*.

John Thayer was a director and second vice-president of the Pennsylvania Railroad Company, and a prominent sportsman in his younger days at cricket and baseball. He lost his life in the sinking.

Jack Thayer was a cricket enthusiast like his father. He was just a teenager when he sailed on the fateful voyage, and only just got off the ship as it was about to go down.

Charles Williams was a successful racquets player. He had won the English Open title in 1911, and the World Championship early in 1912; he was on his way to defend his title in New York.

Leslie Williams was a Welsh bantamweight who had recently got married, and his wife was expecting their second child. He was on his way to a tournament in the United States, and along with fellow Welsh boxer Dai Bowen, he lost his life in the tragedy.

Duane Williams is credited with helping to establish the International Tennis Federation. He lost his life in the disaster when one of the funnels crashed down on him.

Richard Norris Williams was making his name in the sport of lawn tennis. He was travelling with his father on *Titanic* and was on his way to try to enhance his career playing in tennis tournaments before going on to Harvard University. He was threatened with the amputation of his frozen legs, but he worked hard to save them and went on to become one of the best tennis players of his day, even winning an Olympic gold medal.

Hugh Woolner went up to Trinity College in Cambridge in 1885. He was 6 feet 3 inches tall and gained a blue for throwing the hammer against Oxford. He also rowed at Cambridge and played rugby union.

Frederick Wright was the squash court attendant with the victualling crew, for which he received only £1 a week in wages. He lost his life in the disaster and a special concert to commemorate him was held in his hometown of Great Billing, near Northampton.

him which was erected in Treorchy Cemetery. His brother Stephen (1894-1966) wrote the epitaph:

In loving memory of my dear brother David John Bowen.
No more I'll see him in our midst, no more his voice I'll hear,
For death has been and taken away the one I loved so dear.
Twilight and evening bell, and after that the dark,
And may there be no sadness or farewell when it embark.
Some day, some time my eyes shall see thy loving face.
Never shall your memory fade.

Dai Bowen's great-great nephew is David Squires, a cartoonist associated with several football clubs and the *Guardian* newspaper.

William Ernest Carter
Polo, Squash Racquets and Hunting

William Carter was born on 19 June 1875, in Philadelphia. He was the only son of William Thornton Carter (1927-1893), who had been born in Cornwall in England, and had become a highly successful businessman in the coal and iron industry, and his second wife, Cornelia 'Nellie' Miranda (formerly Redington, 1846-1934). They had married in Ohio in 1868. He had an older sister named Helene Redington (1870-1933), and younger sisters named Grace Alice, who only lived for a few months of 1876, and Alice, who was born in 1878. The family lived at 2116 Walnut Street in Philadelphia.

Known as Willie to his family and friends, he attended the University of Pennsylvania, where he was a member of the class of 1896, and Fraternity of Delta Psi (St Anthony Hall), a literary society. However, he dropped out before he had graduated to concentrate on the sports of polo and hunting. He did some work as a stockbroker, and on his father's death in 1893 he inherited a vast fortune.

He became a member of the Bryn Mawr Benedicts Polo Club; the Philadelphia Country Club, which provides various sports facilities, including a championship golf course; the Racquets

Club; and was a member of the Radnor Foxhunting Equestrians in Philadelphia.

On 29 January 1896 he married Lucile Stewart Polk, at the Franklyn Street Presbyterian Church in her hometown of Baltimore. They had children named Lucile Polk (1897-1962) and William Thornton II (1900-1985). They lived mostly in Philadelphia, where they kept a town house at Rittenhouse Square, entertained extensively at their Gwedna home at Bryn Mawr, but summered at their cottage named 'Quatrefoil' on Narragansett Avenue at Newport in Rhode Island.

From about 1907 the Carter family started renting expensive properties in England, and Willie and Lucile had attended the coronation of King George V and Queen Mary on 22 June 1911. Lucile Polk had attended a private girls' boarding school at Wycombe Abbey in Buckinghamshire, and her parents lived at Rotherby Manor House near Melton Mowbray in Leicestershire. They all met in London and travelled to Southampton to board *Titanic*.

Willie is reported to have been: 'much shaken by his experience and his face showed lines of suffering.' He spoke the following poignant words: 'Terrible, terrible. No pen can ever depict and no tongue can ever describe adequately the terrors of our experience. Everywhere was a cold, hopeless despair and grief in its most hellish form. Some were dumb with horror; others beat their breasts like things crazed, and a few laughed hysterically and insanely.'

Two months after the *Titanic* disaster, Willie received a fractured skull while playing for the Bryn Mawr Benedicts Polo Club against the Philadelphia Country Club's B team on 5 June 1912.

It would seem that Willie and Lucile's marriage was already strained, and following their return to Pennsylvania, the pair divorced in 1914, in what was supposed to have been a secret arrangement, although the media soon got hold of it.

According to the *Newport Mercury* at the time of his death, 'He maintained his summer residence at "Quatrefoil" on Narragansett Avenue, and he was a member of the Newport Reading Room. In recent years he has passed much of his time at his farm at Unionville in Pennsylvania, where he was interested in the breeding of prize-winning Black Horn Angus cattle.'

Willie died at Palm Beach in Florida, on 20 March 1940, aged 64, and was buried at the West Laurel Hill Cemetery at Bala Cynwyd in Pennsylvania.

Lucile Stewart Carter
Polo, Harness Racing and Swimming

Lucile Carter was born as Lucile Stewart Polk on 8 October 1875, at Baltimore in Maryland. She was the daughter of William Plunket Stewart Polk (1828-1917), and his wife Louisa Ellen Hought (formerly Anderson, 1844-1933). Her father was a partner in the very successful insurance brokerage of Hopper, Polk and Purnell, of Baltimore, and a descendant of James Knox Polk (1795-1849), who was president of the United States from 1845 to 1849. She was also linked to the Peale family of painters. She had an older brother named Peter, and a younger brother named David.

While still only 17 she was known for her vivacity and style, being described as a 'Baltimore Belle'. She was noted to have been a good athlete, an excellent swimmer, and was known to be quite daring. It was reported that she was the first woman to play polo riding astride the horse instead of side-saddle, and she drove a coach-and-four through a crowded Thomas Street in her home city. She was the first woman in Philadelphia to wear a harem skirt, and was noted for her striking clothes.

On 29 January 1896 she married William Carter, at the Franklyn Street Presbyterian Church in her hometown of Baltimore, and the ceremony was described in local newspapers as, 'One of the social events of the season'.

Alongside a photograph of her, the *Reading Eagle* for 18 June 1914, reported:

> Philadelphia, June 18: Society here, in New York, Newport, Washington, Baltimore and London is wondering if pretty, vivacious and daringly original Mrs William E. Carter, just secretly divorced from her husband, will marry again. The couple were saved from the Titanic disaster with their two children in the same lifeboat with Mrs John Jacob Astor.
>
> As Lucile Polk, daughter of an old Baltimore family and grand-daughter of ex-president Polk, she was one of the beauties of the small but distinguished home coterie. When she met young William E. Carter, dashing polo player and yachtsman, using his vast fortune in healthy pleasure, the conquest was mutual and instant.
>
> Their marriage was a brilliant one. Philadelphia society was the first conquest of the bride. Her fascinating entertainments, spiced with new ideas, were irresistible. Newport found them so. England as well.
>
> Mrs Carter is a noted athlete herself. She was the first woman to play polo riding astride, and the first woman to drive a four-in-hand through crowded Thames Street.

Lucile later married George Clymer Brooke (1867-1953), and had a daughter named Elizabeth Muhlenberg Blake (1916-2016). Lucile died of a heart attack on 26 October 1934, aged 59, at the impressive Almondbury House in Ithan, Delaware County, Pennsylvania, and was buried at St Michael's Cemetery in Birdsboro, Berkshire County, Pennsylvania.

Thornton Davidson

Ice Hockey, Lawn Tennis, Equestrian and Sailing

Thornton Davidson was born on 16 May 1880, the son of Sir Charles Peers Davidson (1841-1929), who was chief justice of the Quebec Supreme Court in Canada, and his wife Alice Harriet (formerly Mattice, 1844-1915). They had seven children, including Peers (1870-1923), a well-known Montreal lawyer; Shirley (1874-1907), who was a prominent forward for the Montreal Victorias ice hockey club; and Campbell 'Cammie' (1877-1940), who also played for the club.

Thornton followed in his brothers' footsteps and played ice hockey for the Montreal Victorias. He took part in other sports, being described as 'a sailor of intrepid and daring and remarkable skill, and he also played lawn tennis and was a good horseman.'

The Stanley Cup is the championship trophy awarded to the National Hockey League Play-Off Champions and was first awarded in 1893. The Montreal Victorias won the title in 1895 and dominated the competition until 1899. The Allan Cup has been awarded to the senior ice hockey champions of Canada since 1909, and the Montreal Victorias were champions in 1911 and 1912.

Thornton was described as 'a young man with a brilliant future ahead of him', when he entered into partnership in a brokerage business as 'Hickson and Davidson'. He bought out his partner in 1908 and became 'Thornton Davidson and Company'.

On 3 November 1906 he married Orian Hays, second daughter of Charles Melville Hays and his wife Clara Jennings Hays, her father being the president of the Grand Trunk Pacific Railway in Montreal.

Sadly, a tragedy hit the family in 1907 when Thornton's brother Shirley and his fiancée Aileen Higston were drowned while out sailing in what was believed to be a suicide pact after Judge Davidson would not agree to them marrying because she was a Roman Catholic.

Thornton's father Charles Hays was the potential victim of a card shark on *Titanic* named George Brereton, who had given his name when boarding as George Brayton. He was a professional gambler and con-man who had with him a list of the first-class passengers he intended to target during the voyage. In particular he had circled the name of Charles Hays and marked it 'millionaire'.

Thornton's body was never identified, but there is a memorial to him at the Mount Royal Cemetery in Montreal. On news of his death, the financial exchange in Montreal opened for only one hour on 25 April 1912 and then closed again as a mark of respect.

Sir Cosmo Edmund Duff-Gordon
Fencing, Martial Arts and Shooting

Cosmo Duff-Gordon was born on 22 July 1862 and was baptised at St George's, Hanover Square, London. He was the eldest of three sons in a family of five children, born between 1861 and 1869, to Cosmo Lewis Duff-Gordon (1812-1876), and Anna Maria (1836-1898), a daughter of Sir Edmund Antrobus, 2nd Baronet, of Antrobus Hall near Mobberley in Cheshire. In 1813, the Baronetcy of Halkin in Aberdeenshire was conferred on his great-great uncle, Sir James Duff, and Cosmo became the 5th Baron of Halkin in 1896. He was educated at Eton College and became a member of the Bath Club and the Automobile Club.

On 7 June 1900 he married the well-known fashion designer Lucy Christiana Sutherland (1863-1935) in Venice. The union was not universally accepted, however, as Lucy was a divorcee, and her sister was Elinor Glyn, a notorious romance writer.

Sir Cosmo was interested in various sports, including Bartitsu, a Japanese martial arts and self-defence method established in England at the turn of the century, by Edward Barton-Wright. The name is derived from the first part of his name (Bar) and the second part of the martial art of Ju-jitsu, which he said meant 'fighting to the last'. Barton-Wright said that the sport comprised of boxing, or the use of the fist as a hitting medium, the use of the feet as a means of offence and defence, and the walking stick as a means of self-defence in such a way as to make it practically impossible to be hit on the fingers. He had established a Bartitsu School of Arms and Physical Culture on Shaftesbury Avenue in London's Soho district, which Sir Cosmo frequented.

Sir Cosmo had also achieved the Olympic standard in fencing and was chosen to represent Britain at the Athens games in 1906, in what was an interim sports festival arranged to celebrate the tenth anniversary of the first Olympic Games held in Athens in 1896.

The fencing events were held at various sites, most of the matches being held outside in an open courtyard at the Zappeion. Under the title 'Brilliant English Fencing' the *Daily Telegraph* for 26 April 1906, reported:

> The English fencing team has reached the final, and has created two records for English sport, namely, that one Englishman, Sir Cosmo Duff Gordon, has hit every Frenchman, and that the English team has fought a dead-heat with the French team in the final. After doing so much more brilliantly than anyone expected, the English team were beaten by France in fighting off the final. They beat Germany by seven and Belgium by five points. With a little better fortune in judging the final they would have won outright.
>
> Mr Seligman did best in all the four fights with twelve hits, counting coups doubles, and only six defeats. Lord Desborough was untouched by the Germans, and Mr Newton Robinson's steadiness produced a victory over Belgium in the adverse circumstances of fatigue and bad light. His hit on the German, Herr Casimir, was especially fine, as was that on the Frenchman, M Dillon-Kavanagh, who was also hit twice by M. Seligman.
>
> Another feature, also unparalleled in an international fencing tournament, was that two cases of dead-heat occurred in the team fight, for France only beat Greece after equality in the first fight, and by two points in the second. The Greeks were finely trained and clever fighters, having practised long and hard for victory.
>
> A very large crowd assembled for the final between England and France, when Sir Cosmo Duff Gordon's success produced equality after his comrades had had very bad luck. The English did not show such good form at the second attempt, losing by three points, but have never been nearer winning an international fight against so many entries.

Sir Cosmo was a member of the committee for the 1908 Olympic Games held in London, having been appointed by Lord Desborough, chairman of the British Olympic Association. He took part in pistol duelling competitions as a member of the British team demonstrating the sport, which was held in the fencing arena.

After the sinking, Sir Cosmo was called to give evidence at the British Wreck Inquiry on Day 10, May 17, and Day 11, May 20. His wife also gave evidence.

Sir Cosmo and Lucy were estranged in 1915 but remained on speaking terms. Bottom of Form

Sir Cosmo died at 5 Alfred Place in South Kensington, London, on 20 April 1931, aged 68, and was buried at Brookwood Cemetery (plot 25) near Woking in Surrey. Lucy died in a Putney nursing home on 20 April 1935, four years to the day after her husband, and is buried with him.

In the 1997 film *Titanic,* Sir Cosmo and Lady Duff-Gordon were portrayed by Martin Jarvis and Rosalind Ayers, who were also a married couple. At the time of the centenary, in 2012, a box marked 'Titanic' containing documents and letters belonging to the couple was discovered in a London legal office.

Francis 'Frank' Dymond
Boxing

Frank Dymond was born on 1 April 1876, at Poole in Dorset, and was baptised at Llanaber near Barmouth in west Wales, on 21 July 1877. Apparently, his surname was a West Country variation of Diamond. He was the elder of three surviving sons (a brother named William Thomas had died as an infant in 1879) in a family of eight children (a sister named Helena had died aged two in 1886), born between 1876 and 1893, to a hawker named William Thomas Dymond, who was born in Exeter in 1855, and his wife Catherine (formerly Brantz, 1855-1904), who had been born in Winchester. A hawker is a type of street vendor who travels around selling goods, and at the time of the 1881 census the family were living at 3 Tuttle Street in Wrexham, north-east Wales (the street still exists). Because of the nature of his father's business, the family moved around from place to place, and it seems they spent much of the 1880s in the Bristol area.

On 10 May 1898 Frank married a Southampton girl named Mary Jane (formerly Lisle, 1881-1971) and their first child named Frank William was born in Southampton in the following year. They went on to have four boys and six girls between 1899 and 1920, their last surviving child being Edward, who died in Southampton in 2000.

Frank joined the Royal Navy as a stoker on 13 July 1897. He was described as being just over 5 feet 7 inches tall, with brown hair, grey eyes, and a dark complexion. He had several tattoos on both arms. His first posting was the shore station Victory II, and he subsequently served on a number of ships, during which time he spent several stretches in cells for misconduct, and received forty-two days' hard labour for deserting his ship, HMS *Good Hope*.

While serving on HMS *Firequeen* Frank's naval career was curtailed on 29 January 1904, when his service was no longer required. However, later in the year he fraudulently re-entered the Royal Navy with the name Frank Davis, but the deception was discovered in May 1905.

The *Hampshire Advertiser* for 16 September 1905, reported that he had appeared at Southampton Police Court charged with abandoning his wife and children; supposedly to look for work. He had promised to send her money but failed to do so. The report stated that he had deserted from the navy some time previously.

Frank decided to turn his attention to the Merchant Navy and joined the White Star Line as a fireman. Described by his family as a 'hard man', he was handy with his fists and used them to take part in boxing bouts on board his ships, with the purse being put up by some of the first-class passengers. While serving on board the White Star Liner *Teutonic* 'he began to give his opponent such a beating that the ship's officers stopped the contest at the end of the sixth round'.

Frank later became involved in professional boxing, and on 16 October 1909 he lost to Jack Kellar of London by a knockout in the third round, at the Empire Theatre in Southampton.

The 1901 census records that the family home was at 29 Dock Street in Southampton, and a decade later they lived at 3 Farmers Court in Southampton. When the RMS *Titanic* came to his city he joined as a fireman/stoker on 10 April 1912, a job for which he would receive £6 a month.

After the sinking he was summoned to be present at the British Board of Trade Titanic Inquiry, and he was paid expenses, but he was not required to give evidence.

During the First World War Frank served on SS *Lapland*, the ship which had brought him back to Britain after the disaster. His brother Edward was aged 34 when he joined the Royal Navy as a stoker first class on 7 December 1915. He served on HMS *Tipperary* during the battle of Jutland on 1 June 1916. After being taken prisoner, Edward died at the Fortress Hospital in Heligoland on the following day and was buried in Hamburg.

At the cease of hostilities, Frank continued his involvement in boxing, taking part in fights and training and seconding upcoming young fighters. His ring career was not particularly impressive, however. He seems to have had the strength and stamina, but was lacking the knock-out punch needed to be a champion boxer. On 6 August 1920, he lost on points in ten rounds to Teddy Murton at the Drill Hall in Southampton. The fight was reported in the *Dundee Courier* for 7 August 1920. In April 1921 he lost on points in ten rounds to Johnny Jones, at the Cosmopolitan Gymnasium in Plymouth. On 2 June 1923 he lost on points in ten rounds to Matt George of Portsmouth at the Southampton Coliseum, which was a major venue in the town.

Although he was interviewed by newspaper reporters soon after the disaster, it is said that he became a heavy drinker and would never talk about the dreadful experience he suffered – not even to his family.

Frank Dymond died after a long illness at his home at 22 Derby Road in the St Mary district of Southampton, on 19 June 1947, aged

71, and was buried with his mother at Southampton Old Cemetery (section A160, plot 182). His wife was buried with them in 1971, and the grave is marked with a wooden cross.

In a 2021 episode of the BBC programme 'The Repair Shop', Frank's logbook was brought in by his great-grandson, where it was re-bound.

Mark Fortune
Curling

Mark Fortune was born at Carluke in Wentworth County, Ontario, Canada, on 2 November 1847. He was the second son of five in a family of ten children, born between 1844 and 1864, to a farmer named Robert Fortune (1821-1888), who originally came from Berwickshire in Scotland, and his wife Elizabeth Bell (formerly Johnston, 1821-1892).

After spending several years in San Francisco, Mark moved to Winnipeg, Manitoba, Canada, in 1871, where he established a real estate business four years later, erecting many buildings on Portage Avenue. He served on the Winnipeg County Council from 1879 to 1881, and again in 1883. He was an active member of the Knox Presbyterian Church, served one term in the Winnipeg School Board in 1878, and was president of the St Andrews Society of Winnipeg, 1897-1898. He was a founder of the Winnipeg Real Estate Board in 1903, and in 1905 was a founding member of the St Charles Country Club.

On 10 November 1876, Mark married Mary McDougald (1851-1929) in Winnipeg, and they had six children: Robert William Hamilton (1877-1965); Clara Alma (1879-1964); Ethel Flora (1883-1961); Alice Elizabeth (1887-1961); Mabel Helen (1888-1968), and Charles Alexander (1892-1912). The family home was at 393 Wellington Crescent in Winnipeg.

Mark was keen on the winter sport of curling, being president of the Granite Curling Club in Winnipeg, from 1894 to 1896. He was remembered as being brash and self-confident, and was considered, 'probably one of the most expert of Winnipeg's curlers. His judgement was sound, his discrimination keen, his life purpose high.' In 1911 he built a large Tudor-style mansion at 393 Wellington Crescent in Winnipeg.

The *Manitoba Free Press* for 20 April 1912, reported:

> Strong and self-contained in the time of great bereavement, the survivors of the Fortune family, Mrs Fortune and her three daughters, Mabel, Ethel and Alice, were joined in their rooms in the Belmont Hotel today by Charles Allen, of Winnipeg, who is engaged to the latter member of the family. But though showing remarkable fortitude, they would talk but little of the terrible tragedy by which they were robbed of father and brother.
>
> This strikes the newspaper man on the *Titanic* wreck assignment as being characteristic of nearly all of the survivors. There is a dread of recalling the awful disaster by talking of it, for the accounting of the events seems at one to bring the dreadful picture before their eyes. To Mr Allan however, the story has been told, in part disjointedly and with little sequence, but still bringing forth many graphic pictures.

Mark Fortune is commemorated by Fortune Street in Winnipeg, and the chimes, which still peel in Winnipeg's Knox United Church, were installed and dedicated to his memory.

Charles Alexander Fortune
Ice Hockey

Charles Fortune was born on 13 October 1892, in Winnipeg, the youngest of six children to Mark and Mary Fortune.

He graduated in 1911 from Bishop's College in Lennoxville, Quebec, with citations for academic and athletic excellence, particularly at ice hockey, and intended to enrol at McGill University in Montreal.

His sister Ethel was haunted by an awful glimpse of Charles, 'in the water, lifejacket on, struggling to stay afloat, and crying for someone to save him.' In reality it was not possible for her to have witnessed the dreadful event, but what she saw in her mind's eye stayed with her for the rest of her life.

Frederick Maxfield Hoyt
Sailing

Frederick Hoyt was born on 15 September 1873, at Stamford in Fairfield County, Connecticut, United States. He was the third son of four, born between 1866 and 1882, to Joseph Blachley Hoyt (1813-1888), and his second wife Susan Swan (formerly Evans, 1837-1907), who was originally from Weymouth in Dorset. Sadly, the fourth brother died as an infant in 1883. His father was a tanner, who became the head of a company of leather merchants named Hoyt Brothers of New York.

Frederick prepared at Berkeley School in New York City. He took the Electrical Engineering Course in college and was a member of Delta Phi. He was on the track team in his freshman year and was vice-commodore of the senior year. He graduated from Sheffield Scientific School, Yale, in 1895, and attended two reunions.

From 1896 to 1906 he was associated with the naval architect William Gardner, and in 1907 became special partner in the firm of Hendrickson, Hall and Company. He was president of the Greenport Basin and Construction Company, Yacht and Ship Builders, and he was a member of the Society of Naval Architects and Marine Engineers. On the 1900 United States census he was listed as a yacht designer of Stamford City.

A noted sailor, he became a member of the well-known prestigious Larchmont Yacht and Country Club in Long Island Sound on 28 June 1899, acting as commodore from 1901 to 1904, vice-commodore from 1906 to 1907, and also served on the race committee from 1915 to 1932. Later he joined the New York Yacht Club. He owned several prestigious yachts, including *Norota, Syce* and *Isolde.*

In 1905 he was navigator on the schooner yacht *Atlantic*, which beat ten other yachts to win the international ocean race known as the

Kaiser's Cup. It started at Sandy Hook in New Jersey and finished at Lizard's Point in Cornwall, and the vessel took an impressive twelve days and four hours to complete the course. The time stood as the record for over 100 years, making it the longest lasting record in the history of sport.

Frederick married Jane Anne Forby (1879-1932) on 17 May 1906, at Manhattan in New York. He maintained a summer home at Stamford and also spent time at Marblehead in Massachusetts.

Working as a broker, at the time of the *Titanic* disaster he had premises at 71 Broadway, while he and Jane lived at 112 East Seventy-Third Street in Manhattan.

He and his wife spent their last years living at the Manor Inn at Larchmont, Mamaranek Town, Westchester County, New York State, United States. They lived at some time in the Los Angeles area, and his wife died at Long Beach in California. He suffered with pneumonia, which brought on a heart attack, and like Harry Anderson, he died at the New Rochelle Hospital in New York, on 5 July 1940, aged 66, and was buried with his wife at Woodland Cemetery in Stamford.

Joseph Bruce Ismay
Lawn Tennis, Shooting, Golf, Motoring and Fishing

Bruce Ismay was born on 12 December 1862, at Enfield House on Endbutt Lane in the Great Crosby district to the north of Liverpool. He was the eldest son of five and the second child of eleven, born between 1860 and 1874, of Thomas Henry Ismay (1837-1899), a senior partner in the shipping firm of Ismay, Imrie, and Company, and a founder of the White Star Line, and his wife Margaret Bruce (1837-1907). They had married on 7 April 1859, at St Bride's Church in the Canning district of Liverpool.

In 1865 the family moved to a substantial mansion on the banks of the River Mersey at 15 Beach Lawn in Waterloo, Liverpool, which is now a grade II listed building and displays a blue plaque dedicated to Thomas Ismay. It is said that White Star liners used to sound their horns as they passed by the house. In 1885, the family moved to a mansion called 'Dawpool' near Thurstaston on the Wirral in Cheshire.

The anti-establishment London newspaper *Reynold's* for 21 April 1912 reported on the Ismay family under the title 'A Survivor of the Titanic':

> In this column, where as a rule we write only of the living, we may speak of Joseph Bruce Ismay. Mr Ismay, who is in his fiftieth year, was born in Liverpool. He is chairman and managing director of the White Star Line. He is president and member of the British committee of the International Mercantile Marine Company, which was incorporated in 1893 under the laws of New Jersey. He is also, with several other company associations, a director of the London and North-Western Railway. But it is more to our present purpose to say that he is one of the survivors of the *Titanic*.
>
> Ismay is a rare name. We fancy it is not to be found anywhere outside the north-west of England. It was the name of a lady living in the time of King Edward I, who is claimed as an ancestress of Mr Ismay. The first to make the name widely known was Mr Ismay's father, the late Thomas Henry Ismay, who, coming out of Maryport in Cumberland, became a shipping prince in Liverpool. It was in 1868 that he established, in conjunction with William Imrie, the company which has since become famous as the White Star Line. It was for him that was built the first vessel to have her saloon accommodation mid-ships.
>
> Joseph Bruce Ismay is the eldest of three brothers, and appears to be the only one who is actively associated with shipping. He has two sons and two daughters, his wife being the eldest daughter of George R Schieffelin of New York. His youngest brother, Charles Bowen, married her sister. The other brother, James Hainsworth Ismay, married into the English aristocracy. He is now lying seriously ill with pneumonia at Iwerne Minster House in Dorsetshire. One of the sisters is the wife of Mr Geoffrey Drags, who used to be MP for Derby.
>
> Joseph Bruce Ismay is an Old Harrovian; shoots, motors and golfs; and is a member of the Reform Club. He has a house at Thurstaston on the Dee near Birkenhead, another at Mossley Hill in Liverpool, and another in Hill Street. There are plenty of Hill Streets, but the

> one we mean is the fashionable street which runs out of Berkeley Square, a street where only 'nobs' live.

Bruce was sent to board at Seafield School in New Brighton, a private preparatory school for boys aged between 8 and 13, where he was listed on the 1871 census returns. Then he went to Elstree School at Hill House on Elstree Hill, now a BUPA care centre, before he went to Harrow in 1877. However, he only remained at Harrow for a year, and instead of going on to study at university as might be expected, he was sent to a private tutor at Dinard in Brittany.

He was apprenticed to his father's firm for four years after which he toured the world, and then went to New York City as the company representative and agent. In 1891 he was made a partner in his father's firm.

In addition to shooting, motoring and playing golf, as previously mentioned, he was also a talented lawn tennis player who won the Waterloo Championships in Liverpool, and the Northern Mixed Doubles Championships at Manchester in 1883, which was later moved to the All England Club at Wimbledon; and the Northumberland Championships in Newcastle in 1884.

He also went on tour to Australia, and under the title: 'Inter-Colonial Lawn Tennis Championships' the *Sydney Morning Herald* for 30 April 1885, reported:

> At 11 o'clock to-day the inter-colonial lawn tennis match between New South Wales and Victoria, commences at the Association Cricket Ground, Moore Park, and a very exciting contest is expected, both teams being in good form. The play of the Victorians has been much admired by the spectators, who have been looking on during the last two days. Some very good courts have been prepared, and the arrangements for the comfort of visitors have been sedulously looked after by the committee. Luncheon will be obtainable on the ground. Play every day will cease about 4.30. Mr. J. Bruce Ismay, of the Northern Lawn Tennis Association, England, has kindly consented to act as referee during the match.

Mr Salmon and Mr Ismay had never even practised together before the tournament, and the *Sydney Morning Herald* for 8 May 1885, reported on the final of the Inter-Colonial Men's Doubles Championship of New South Wales, in which 'Mr Salmon and Mr Ismay beat Mr Riddell and Mr Coldham 7-5, 6-4, 3-6, 4-6, 7-5...This was a very good match. Mr Salmon and Mr Ismay won the first two sets, buy lost the third and fourth, and in the final set the Victorian pair had four games to three called in their favour, the set ultimately being five games all; and vantage games being played, Mr Salmon and Mr Ismay just won.'

In New York City on 4 December 1888, Bruce married Julia Florence Schieffelin of a wealthy New York family, and they had four children who survived infancy: Margaret Bruce in 1889; Thomas Bruce in 1894; Evelyn Constance in 1897 and George Bruce in 1902. Henry Bruce died as an infant in 1891, and another child is believed to have died in infancy in 1900. Bruce's brother Charles Bower married Julia's sister, Matilda Constance, in 1904. They lived at a house called 'Sandheys' on Mossley Hill Road, Liverpool.

In an article for the *Brooklyn Daily Eagle*, under the title: 'Men and Women Helped into First Lifeboats by White Star Director', it was stated that Karl Behr, '...lauds Mr Ismay for his generalship and help in saving many people.'

Behr continued:

> Mr Ismay himself directed the launching splendidly [of the second lifeboat, number 5]; before getting in. However, Mrs Beckwith turned to him and asked if the men folk could come too, and he said, 'Why certainly'. We got into the boat, and then Mr Ismay asked if there was anybody else to get in and there was no one at all left around there.
>
> Fully three minutes we waited for others to come along before he gave orders to launch the boat, having sent in two petty officers and two or three seamen. The latter were under perfect control. Fortunately for us, when we left the ship, everything was handled in the most perfect manner and discipline, thanks to Mr Ismay, he made sure that our crew was complete.

As *Titanic* went down, Mr Ismay is said to have kept his back to the ship and cried. While on board *Carpathia* he was taken to the cabin of the ship's doctor, Frank McGee, and remained there for the entire journey to New York. Apparently, someone had placed a sign on the door saying, 'Don't Knock'. He could not eat anything solid and was kept under the influence of opiates to calm him down. Jack Thayer visited him and tried to console him, even though he had just lost his father. He stated that Mr Ismay, '...was staring straight, shaking like a leaf. Even when I spoke to him he paid absolutely no attention. I have never seen a man so completely wrecked.'

Mr Ismay was called to give evidence at the United States Senate Inquiry on Day 11, 30 April, being 'grilled' twice, and then at the British Wreck Inquiry on Day 16, 4 June, and Day 17, 5 June.

On his return to England, London newspapers for 11 May 1912, reported: 'Mr Joseph Bruce Ismay, managing director of the White Star Line, arrived in Liverpool on Saturday. His treatment in the United States in connection with the *Titanic* disaster, of which he was a survivor, was remembered by the large assemblage on the wharf. When he appeared at the head of the gangway he was loudly cheered.'

Stewardess Sarah Stap, who was also qualified as a nurse, had been born on board her own father's ship, and had been at sea for twelve years. She was rescued in lifeboat 11 and therefore was in a good position to witness what Mr Ismay did. She stated:

> I think it is most unfair the stories that have been circulated about Mr Ismay. He worked might and main all the time, and I did not think he actually realised the ship was sinking. He helped all he could to get the women into the boats. He implored one group of stewardesses to take their place with the others. The reply was: 'But we are only stewardesses, sir!' When he said: 'You are women. Please get in at once.' And he insisted on their doing so. We saw him later when he was sitting on the gunwale of one of the last boats to leave. He had nothing on but his pyjamas and an overcoat and he was blue with the cold.

However, although Bruce was cleared of any direct blame for the disaster, he was savaged in the American and British Press, who gave him the unsympathetic name of 'J. Brute Ismay'. He was ostracised, and even attacked, and both he and Julia were often abused when they were out in public. The dark shadow of the *Titanic* disaster never ceased to haunt him.

Bruce's brother, Captain Charles Ismay, was a successful horse trainer, and just before the *Titanic* disaster his horse Bloodstone was second in the Grand National, and his horse Jacobus was second in the 1915 Grand National. However, his most famous horse was Craganour. As the Derby of 1913 drew near, Craganour became a strong public favourite. There were two sensational incidents in the race, for not only was the King's horse, Anmer, brought down by a suffragist at Tattenham Corner, but after finishing first in the race, Craganour's number was hoisted as the winner, only to be followed by his disqualification, the race being awarded to Aboyeur. The disqualification aroused a vast amount of discussion, but none of the Stewards ever gave any explanation of the grounds on which the decision was decided. However, it was widely thought that it was due to his connection with his brother.

During his life Bruce was an official of several insurance companies. He was chairman of the Asiatic Steam Navigation Company; the Liverpool Steamship Owners Protection Association; the Liverpool and London War Risk Association; the Birmingham Canal Navigation Company; and the London and Scottish Railway.

He retired from public life on 30 June 1913, and for the remainder of his life he became a virtual recluse. He and Julia spent much of their time on the west coast of Ireland, enjoying the tranquillity of the countryside around Costelloe Lodge on the banks of the River Casla in Connemara, County Galway, where he took up fishing. Irish nationalists burned the Ismay home to the ground in 1922, and they had it re-built by the respected architect and designer of country houses, Edwin Lutyens. They also kept a house at 15 Hill Street, one of the more prestigious streets in the affluent district of Mayfair in west London.

In the garden of Costelloe Lodge is a limestone memorial dedicated to Ismay, which reads: 'He loved all wild and solitary places where we taste the pleasure of believing what we see is boundless as we wish our souls to be.'

Bruce Ismay's health fell into decline in the 1930s after being diagnosed with diabetes. When the disease caused the amputation of his right leg below the knee, he became confined to a wheelchair. On the morning of 14 October 1937, he suffered a massive stroke and collapsed in his bedroom at his residence in Mayfair, which left him unconscious, blind and unable to speak. He died on 17 October 1937, aged 74. His funeral was held at St Paul's Church in Knightsbridge, and he was buried in Putney Vale Cemetery in London. Julia died in Kensington in 1963 and was buried with her husband.

Some newspapers reported on his death under the title: 'An Echo of the *Titanic* – Death of Bruce Ismay.' They continued to be unsympathetic concerning the disaster, and ridiculously inaccurate, seemingly getting parts of the report mixed-up with Sir Cosmo Duff-Gordon and his wife:

> In 1912 the *Titanic* made its first and last voyage. The ship was the latest addition to the White Star Line, and was reported by the designers as unsinkable.
>
> At noon on 12 April 1912, the *Titanic* left Southampton for New York. There were 2,500 passengers and a crew of 860 officers and men under the command of Captain E.J. Smith.
>
> Joseph Bruce Ismay, who was managing director of the White Star Line, was a passenger on the maiden voyage of the *Titanic*. Among the passengers were some of the wealthiest citizens of the United States. The ship went down in mid-ocean with a loss of 1,635 lives. A great proportion of these being passengers in the cheaper class.
>
> At the inquiry there were some very startling statements given in evidence. It was stated that the wireless officer had reported that icebergs were in the vicinity. The speed of the gigantic vessel was not reduced. Statements were made that Bruce Ismay had instructed Captain Smith not to reduce speed. The ship struck an iceberg and had a tremendous length ripped out of the side.

At the time quite a number of the passengers were enjoying themselves at a ball. When some became anxious they were told there was no danger as the ship could not possibly sink owing to its special construction. When Captain Smith realised that the ship was in grave danger he ordered the boats to be lowered. A panic ensued, it was stated by the third-class passengers who had obtained access to the main boat deck. Several men who tried to rush the boats were shot down by the officers.

Evidence was given by a steward that Bruce Ismay and his wife, with two or three other passengers, were in their boat, and that Bruce Ismay had offered them a large reward if he and his wife were saved. This lifeboat was pulled away from the wreck almost empty.

One cannot quite realise the terrible scene when all the boats had left, and nearly two thousand people remained aboard with no hope of rescue. Those in the boats heard the doomed ones singing 'Nearer My God To Thee.' Captain Smith went down with his ship.

At the conclusion of the inquiry Bruce Ismay was exonerated from blame for the sinking of the ship. It had been stated that he had instructed the Captain not to reduce speed when the bergs were reported, as they were after the record.

Bruce Ismay was not exonerated for cowardice. So bitter were the people that when he was seen in the street they would follow him with execrations and shriek the word 'coward' at him. He and his wife were ostracised.

Bruce Ismay lived like a hermit. He had plenty of money, but his life was a misery. He recently died in London, at the age of 74, and his death has brought back the tragic memory of the ill-fated *Titanic*.
Bottom of Form

Thomas McCawley

Gymnastics, Fencing and Football

Originally thought to have been born in Aberdeen, Thomas McCawley was born on 22 November 1871, at the Union Workhouse, a large complex on Eccles New Road in Salford. He was baptised at the Cathedral Church of St John the Evangelist on Chapel Street in Salford, on 3 December 1871.

His birth certificate states his mother as Jane McAuley, a flax spinner. The 1871 census records a Jane McCawley or McAuley, residing in Pendleton, Salford. She had been born in Belfast and was married to Belfast-born Thomas McCauley (both born in about 1845). They had daughters named Margaret (born in 1866), and Emma (born in 1868).

He was still residing in the workhouse at the time of the 1881 census, until he started work as a collier (probably at Agecroft Colliery), and a decade later he was still a collier, living at the home of Edward Hughes and his family, at 89 Pendlebury Road in Swinton.

On 4 January 1887, newspapers reported that he had suffered a 'Murderous Assault' at the hands of a father and son named Muldoon during a wake after a funeral. When the pair were arrested and taken to the infirmary to be identified, he was in such a critical condition that he could not see them and only recognised their voices, remarking, 'You have done for me.'

On 16 May 1892, aged 21, Thomas went to the Cross Lane Infantry Barracks in Salford and joined the 3rd Battalion, Manchester Regiment, being described as just under 5 feet 4 inches tall and weighing 145 pounds. He had brown hair, grey eyes and a fresh complexion. His religion was given as Wesleyan.

He spent his first years serving at home and taking part in army sports. In December 1895 he was awarded a first-class certificate in gymnastics, and a first-class certificate in fencing in July 1896.

On 31 October 1896, having been promoted to corporal, Thomas refereed a notorious Aldershot League football match at the Queen's Parade Ground between the 2nd Gordon Highlanders and the Royal Irish Rifles. The match turned into a brawl and he was mobbed by supporters of the Irish unit. Corporal McCawley reported the incident to the emergency committee at Aldershot, who suspended the Irish for just a week, recommending that future games should be roped off, and higher-ranking men should take charge.

Thomas was posted to Gibraltar in November 1897 and rose to the rank of quartermaster sergeant. In August 1899, as 3645 Sergeant

McCawley, he sailed from Gibraltar to the Cape of Good Hope with the 1st Battalion, Manchester Regiment, for active service against Boer commando units in the Second Anglo-Boer War. At the end of the war, he purchased his discharge for £18 on 13 September 1902 and received the Queen's South Africa Medal with Defence of Ladysmith clasp, as well as the King's South Africa Medal with 1901 and 1902 clasps. He stayed on in South Africa, where he established a gymnastics school in Pretoria. However, described as a physical instructor, he arrived in Southampton aboard the *Saxon* on 13 January 1912, where he resided at 22 Camden Place.

In his book *The Truth about Titanic*, written soon after the disaster, Colonel Archibald Gracie stated:

> One of the characters of the ship, best known to us all, was the gymnasium attendant, TW McCawley. He, also, expected me to make my first appearance for a real good exercise on the morrow, but, he, too, was swallowed up by the sea. How well we survivors remember this sturdy little man in white flannels and with his broad English accent! With at tireless enthusiasm he showed us the mechanical devices under his charge and urged us to take advantage of the opportunity of using them, going through the motions of bicycle racing, rowing, boxing, camel and horseback riding, etc.

Clarence Moore
Equestrian and Sailing

Clarence Moore (not to be confused with the writer Clarence Bloomfield Moore) was born on 1 March 1865, at Clarksburg in Harrison County, West Virginia, the eldest son of a legal clerk named Jasper Yates Moore (1834-1907), and his wife Frances Elizabeth (formerly Reynolds, 1842-1894), who were both natives of Virginia. He had a younger brother named Frank.

Clarence was educated at Dufferin College in London, Ontario, and remained in Harrison County until 1890, when he moved to Washington DC. He became interested in exploring and developing various West Virginia coal mining, oil, and timber properties, and in 1891 he became associated with William B. Hibbs and Company in the formation of the banking and brokerage firm of that name. He raised cattle and horses on his farmland at Montgomery County in Maryland, and had some real estate interests in Virginia.

Clarence married Alice McLaughlin, a daughter of the former owner of the *Philadelphia Times*, and they had two children named Frances Sara Preston, born in Pennsylvania in 1894, and Samuel Preston, born in Colombia in 1897. However, Alice died on 17 July 1897, just twelve days after the birth of Samuel.

On 20 June 1900, at Beverley in Massachusetts, Clarence married Maybelle Florence Swift, heiress of Chicago meat packer Edwin C. Swift. They had four children: Edwin in 1901 (who died aged five); Jasper in 1905; Clarence Junior in 1910, who was educated at Eton and Harvard; and Lloyd in 1911.

In 1906 he began to have a large home built at 1746 Massachusetts Avenue in Washington DC, and Clarence Moore House was completed in 1909. He employed twenty servants. The building is now the Uzbekistan Embassy.

According to the *New York Times* for 16 April 1912, 'Socially he [Clarence] is one of the best known men in Washington.' He was a good sailor, being a member of the New York Yacht Club. He also came to be known as one of the finest horsemen in Washington DC, playing an integral part in the establishment of the Chevy Chase Equestrian (Fox Hunting) Club, which had a private golf course and other sporting facilities. He was a master of foxhounds for the Loudon County Hunt, at the new Rock Creek Hunt Club in Leesburgh, Virginia. A member of the Club said of him, 'Clarence Moore the most daring horseman I have ever seen, and yet one could not call him reckless. He knew every phase of foxhunting, which was his greatest hobby.'

Clarence was also a member of a number of private clubs, including the Metropolitan, Alibi, and Chevy Chase, all in Washington; and the Travellers Club in Paris.

He left Washington on 16 March 1912 for what his wife said was a pleasure trip to England, and did not return (see page XX).

Arthur Godfrey Peuchen
Sailing

Arthur Godfrey Peuchen was born on 18 April 1859, in Montreal, Canada East. He was the oldest son of three in a family of six children, born between 1857 and 1868, to a Prussian railroad contractor named Godfrey Emanuel Peuchen (1827-1876), and his wife Eliza Eleanor (formerly Clark, 1828-1912). His father had worked as a railway contractor in South America, before moving to Canada in 1850 to work on the Grand Trunk Railway; becoming a wine merchant in 1858. His Prussian-born maternal grandfather had managed the London Brighton and Midland Railway in England until 1871, when he moved to Toronto.

Arthur was educated in private schools in Ontario and England. His business career began in Toronto in about 1880, as a clerk and salesman, and by 1882 he had started to manufacture paint. The following year he became manager of the Canada Paint Company, where his brother Stanley Cooper was superintendant. The company was the first to specialise in pre-mixed, colour-blended paints.

In 1888 Arthur was commissioned as a lieutenant in the Queen's Own Rifles of Canada. He was promoted captain in 1894, and major in 1904. He was marshalling officer in charge of the Indian Cavalry at the coronation of King George V and Queen Mary in 1911.

Arthur owned a yacht named *Vreda,* which crossed the Atlantic under its own canvas, and won many races in North America and Britain. For a time, he was vice commodore and rear commodore of the Royal Canadian Yacht Club.

The *Sporting Chronicle* for 3 July 1891, reported: 'The yachts Oriole, Aileen, and Vreda, of Toronto, and the White Wings and Verve of Hamilton, started on 1 July in the race for the cup given by her Majesty the Queen, to be sailed for by any Canadian yacht belonging to any recognised club. The course was over 30 miles, on Lake Ontario. The yacht Vreda won after a close and exciting race.'

On 26 April 1893 Arthur married Margaret Thompson in York Township, Ontario, and they had a daughter named Jessie Thompson, born in Toronto in 1894, and a son named Godfrey Alan, born in Toronto in 1897. They owned a vast Victorian estate and mansion called 'Woodlands' at Kempenfelt Bay near Barry, just north of Toronto, which included a marina, tennis courts and riding stables.

In 1897 Arthur perfected plans for extracting chemicals from coarse hardwoods and waste woods used by dyeing industries, wheat growers, and in the manufacture of high explosives like cordite. He subsequently became president of Standard Chemical, Iron and Lumber Company of Canada Limited, with refineries in Montreal, France, Germany and London.

After the sinking he was the only Canadian called to give evidence at the United States Senate Inquiry, which he did on Day 4, 22 April, where he was critical of the captain and the crew, which he said, 'was what we would call in yachting terms a scratch crew, brought from different vessels. They might be the best, but they had not been accustomed to working together.'

He received some criticism as a man who survived, owing to the 'women and children first' rule. However, some newspapers reported, 'Major Peuchen, of the Queen's Own Rifles (Canada) was saved off the *Titanic*, but knowing the value to a soldier of a reputation free from the taint of cowardice he carries with him the following certificate: "Major Arthur Peuchen was ordered into the boat by me owing to the fact that I required a seaman (which he proved to be) as well as a brave man. (Signed) C H Lightoller, second officer, late steamship Titanic."'

Arthur was promoted to lieutenant colonel with the Queen's Own Rifles on 21 May 1912, and received the Volunteer Officers'

Decoration. During the First World War he retired from Standard Chemical in November 1915 to command the Home Battalion of the Queen's Own Rifles.

After the war he lost most of his fortune through making bad investments, but he managed to retain his home until 1928, as well as an apartment in London. He spent the last years of his life living at Hinton in Yellowhead County, in the foothills of Alberta. Colonel Arthur Peuchen died in Toronto on 7 December 1929, aged 70, and was buried at the Mount Pleasant Cemetery in Toronto.

In 1987 his wallet was recovered from the area around the wreck of *Titanic,* in which were streetcar tickets, a traveller's cheque, and his calling card.

Washington Augustus Roebling II
Motor Sports and American Football

Washington Roebling was born on 25 March 1881, at Trenton in Mercer County, New Jersey, United States, to Charles Gustavus Roebling (1849-1918), and Sarah Mahon (formerly Ormsby, 1855-1887), who came from Pittsburgh. His grandfather was John Augustus Roebling (1806-1869), a German-born American civil engineer who made his money from designing and building wire rope bridges and who was the chief engineer on the construction of the Niagara Falls Bridge in 1852. Washington's father, along with his uncle and namesake, Washington Augustus Roebling (1837-1926), who had fought at the battle of Gettysburg during the American Civil War, became civil engineers with the company of John A. Roebling and Sons, and worked on the construction of the Brooklyn Bridge for their father. The bridge was opened on 24 May 1883. He had an older brother named Harrison Ormsby, who died at the age of 5, an older sister named Emily Margaretta, and a younger sister named Helen; all born at Trenton.

Washington attended the elite Hill School at Pottstown in Pennsylvania, a feeder school for Princeton University. At that time the school took part in shinney, town ball, cricket and American football, and Washington excelled at the latter. However, his fascination with motor cars prompted him to join the pioneers of the early days of motor sport.

Just before Christmas 1906, an interesting article was published under the title, 'Bridge Contractor Stricken', which stated:

> Bridges also claim their victims. The Brooklyn Bridge was a particularly fatal structure. Washington A. Roebling, who, after his father's death, took charge of the work, became paralysed from caisson fever. He never fully recovered.
>
> The human wrecks from the same disease turned out from the work of erecting the great span were so numerous that in this manner the terrible disease first became recognised. Some of these wrecks may still be seen in New York. Looking at their pitiful distorted forms, it is difficult to think that once these were strong men, powerful in frame.

Indeed, Mr Roebling struggled against this physical disability to get the bridge finished. Caisson disease, also known as decompression sickness, usually suffered by divers, would have been caused by having to dive into the river to excavate and secure the suspension towers to the bed of the East River.

Under the heading: '140 Miles an Hour Motor Car' the *American Register* for 17 October 1908, reported: 'Mr Washington A. Roebling, the well-known engineer, is experimenting at Trenton, New Jersey, with an automobile constructed of Krupp steel, which is expected to attain a speed of 140 miles an hour. It is stated that the machine, which is designed for military use, has actually reached that speed in its trials.'

In 1909, Washington arranged to take over the Walter Automobile Company because of its mounting financial problems. It was moved to an abandoned brewery owned by the Kuser family at Hamilton in New Jersey, not far from Trenton. Washington's father was made president, and he was made general manager of the new enterprise, the Mercer Automobile Company, which marketed itself to the high end and racing markets.

He worked with noted French auto designer Etienne Planche, designing the Roebling-Planche Racing Car which performed well in auto races of the time. Roebling tested all Mercer models before they entered market and participated in racing.

On 11 November 1910, Washington finished second in a sixteen-lap road race in Savannah, Georgia, in a Mercer car, which is sometimes wrongly recorded as being for the Vanderbilt Cup.

He was returning from a motoring tour of Europe when he lost his life on *Titanic*. His name is commemorated on the family memorial at Riverview Cemetery in Trenton.

Arthur Larned Ryerson
Golf

Arthur Ryerson was born in Chicago, Illinois, on 12 January 1851. He was the elder of two sons in a family of four children, born between 1851 and 1865, to Joseph Turner Ryerson (1813-1883) and his wife Ellen Griffin (formerly Larned, 1827-1881). They had married on 25 October 1858.

Arthur was prepared for college at General Russell's Collegiate and Commercial Institute in New Haven, Connecticut. He went up to the University of Chicago in 1872 and Columbia University in 1873, from where he received the degree of Bachelor of Laws. He practised law in Chicago until 1900, being a partner in a law firm. He was also CEO of the Joseph T. Ryerson and Son Steel Company. From 1883 he was hereditary member of the Society of the Cincinnati in the State of New Jersey, having been proposed by his grandfather, Thomas.

On 31 January 1889 he married Emily Borie of Philadelphia and spent much time at his country place at Springfield Center in Otsego County, New York. However, he also spent a lot of time living in England, France and Italy.

The couple had five children, whom they raised while living at Haverford in Pennsylvania, and they spent their summers at Ringwood Manor at the north end of Otsego Lake in Cooperstown, New York. Their son Arthur Larned Junior was killed in a motor car accident at Bryn Mawr near Philadelphia on 8 April 1912.

Arthur was the owner of the Otsego Golf Club at Cooperstown in New York, from 1901 until his death, and was one of the two western delegates who went to New York in 1895 to assist in forming the United States Golf Association.

He was president and trustee of St Luke's Hospital in Chicago for twenty years, and for twelve years was a member of the General Convention of the Protestant Episcopal Church, and for eighteen years a member of the general board of missions of that church.

After the disaster, his wife Emily sent an affidavit to the United States Senate Inquiry, which was read out on Day 16, 16 May 1912. He is twice commemorated: a memorial at Lakewood Cemetery in Cooperstown and a stone memorial at Graceland Cemetery in Chicago. Both have inscribed in them 'Lux Perpetua Luceat Ep' – May the Light Shine Forever.

John Borie 'Jack' Ryerson
Golf

John Ryerson was born on 16 December 1898, in Chicago, Illinois. He was the youngest of five children to Arthur Larned Ryerson and his wife Emily.

His main interest was golf, and he later bought the Otsego Golf Club in 1930. He was a championship golfer and was reported to have played on more than 1,015 different courses by 1954. His accomplishment was even featured in *Ripley's Believe It or Not*. He eventually increased that number to over 1,400 courses by the end of his life. During his golf career he played with such greats as Bobby Jones, Julius Boros, Gene Littler and Babe Zaharias.

In its 'Golfing Jottings' the *Sydney Morning Herald* for 25 January 1941, reported, 'Jack Ryerson, the runner-up in the 1939 North and South amateur championship, has played on more than 500 courses in Europe and the United States. Of an old golfing family of Chicago, Ryerson's father was one of the two western delegates who went to New York in 1895 to assist in forming the United States Golf Association.'

Jack and his sister Emily, then Mrs Cooke, were invited guests to the film set for the 1953 Hollywood film *Titanic*, and two years later he helped Walter Lord with research for his book, *A Night to Remember*. In 1962 he was interviewed for the 50th anniversary of the disaster, and again in 1972 and 1982.

On 12 April 1963, aged 65, he married 54-year-old Jane Morris at Bethesda-by-the-Sea Episcopal Church, Palm Beach in Florida. They had no children.

By the mid-1980s Jack was diagnosed with early stages of dementia, which developed into Alzheimer's disease. He was admitted to the Noreen McKeen nursing facility in West Palm Beach. Just four months after the *Titanic*'s discovery was broadcast to the world, Jack passed away on 21 January 1986, aged 87. Jane later said, 'He was eating his lunch and then simply closed his eyes and stopped breathing. It was very peaceful.' He was the last surviving member of his family who had been aboard the great ship. Jane died on 15 March 1990 and the couple are buried together at Lakewood Cemetery.

Peter Sloan
Football and Swimming

Peter Sloan was born in Liverpool on 13 February 1881, the son of a travelling draper named Alexander Sloan, and his wife Jane 'Jeanie' McMillan, who were both Scottish, and had married on 11 March 1880 at the Shaw Street Presbyterian Church in the West Derby district of Liverpool. At the time of the April 1881 census, they lived at 9 Brownlow Street, Liverpool. His mother died on 10 November

1881, aged 38, and his father never re-married, before he died on 16 April 1893, aged 40, leaving Peter as an orphan at the age of 12. He continued to live at 16 Brownlow Street, first with his father, and then with his aunt and uncle.

Peter received his education at the Liverpool Institute and served his apprenticeship as a civil engineer at C.S. Wilson and Company of Regent Road in Bootle, Liverpool. He was living at 103 Vine Street, when he joined the White Star Line just two weeks after completing his apprenticeship, and served on various vessels on the Atlantic and Mediterranean routes. He is known to have served as an electrician on the *Celtic,* and then the *Cretic* from 1905 to 1907. He was promoted to chief engineer on board *Laurentic,* and was serving on *Olympic* when she collided with HMS *Hawke.*

Peter enjoyed football and swimming, being a member of the Valkyrie Football Club, which was quite successful in the Liverpool area at the turn of the nineteenth century. During his employment with a number of the White Star ships in the Western and Mediterranean trades he won the half-mile championship for swimming during the Italy versus England gala at Spezia, and the gold medal and silver cup.

On the early morning of 23 January 1909, while sailing from New York to Gibraltar, and carrying over 1,700 passengers, RMS *Republic* was sailing in thick fog when it collided with the Italian liner *Florida* in the vicinity of the Nantucket lightship. The captain was a fellow Liverpudlian named Joseph Barlow Ranson, who used submarine bells, depth-sounding and wireless technology, the first marine rescue made possible by radio, to locate the drifting, stricken *Republic.* Engineer Sloan volunteered for rescue work, for which he received a silver medal.

On 18 August 1908 Peter married Annie Blair at the Fortwilliam Park Church in Belfast. They had no children. At the time of the 1911 census, they were living at 14 Newcastle Road in Wavertree, Liverpool, and when he signed on *Titanic,* as a marine electrical engineer, he gave his address as 77a Clovelly Road in Southampton. He was described as a marine electrical engineer.

Under the title 'Fear Jersey City Girl's Fiancé Went Down with the Titanic', the *Jersey Journal* for 23 April 1912 published the following unexplained article:

> A few hours after the *Titanic* with hundreds of her passengers and crew went down to their ocean grave, a letter was received in this city by Miss Sara Weir of 173 Clendenny Avenue, from her sweetheart, Peter Sloan, chief electrician of the ill-fated steamer. It carried an invitation to Miss Weir to visit 'The Queen of the Seas' on Wednesday last, when she was due to arrive in New York.
>
> Mr Sloan, it would seem, went down with his vessel, and it is believed stuck to his post to the last, caring for the oil engines that ran the dynamos that ran the ship's lights and telephones. Had the lights gone out before they did – and they were shining until a few moments before the *Titanic* plunged beneath the waves, the horror of the disaster would have been far greater than it was.
>
> Miss Weir is almost prostrated at the news of her affianced's death, though she feels yet that he might possibly have been saved by some fishing vessel. When the bodies recovered by the *Mackay-Bennett* come to New York she will try to see if that of her lover is among them.
>
> Mr Sloan had been employed by the White Star Line for several years, and prior to being assigned to the *Titanic* just after her launch in Belfast several months ago, was second electrician of her sister ship, RMS *Olympic*. He was elated over his new position on the *Titanic*, which was a promotion, and was proud of being on the largest and finest vessel afloat.
>
> He had visited this city several times, and wrote that he was bringing over to Miss Weir several Christmas gifts. Mr Sloan was a fine manly man just in his thirties, a graduate of an English college, and an all-round athlete and swimmer. He had won several medals for swimming, and this fact leaves Miss Weir, 'hoping against hope,' to think he may have some way kept afloat and been saved. Had he been rescued, however, by the *Carpathia*, he would undoubtedly have communicated with his friends here. His name does not appear on the lists of survivors.
>
> Mr Sloan was born in Scotland, but his parents died when he was a child and he had no immediate relatives living. That he died like a hero – if he is dead – is Miss Weir's conviction, and that is the

> conviction of all who know the young man whose prospects in life were so bright less than ten days ago.

Peter's estate was administered to Annie, who never remarried, and she lived at 17 Ferndale Road in Waterloo, Liverpool, when she died in 1925.

He is named on a brass memorial plaque situated at the Church of St Faithful in Crosby, Liverpool, which is dedicated to the chief engineer and his engine room staff; on the Liverpool Titanic Engineers Memorial; on the Engineers Memorial at East Park in Southampton; on the Glasgow Institute of Marine Engineers Memorial; on the London Institute of Marine Engineers Memorial; and he is mentioned on the memorial stone at the grave of his parents at Anfield Cemetery in Liverpool, which reads, originally in capital letters:

> In Affectionate Remembrance of Jeanie McMillan, the beloved wife of Alexander Sloan, who died 10 November 1881, aged 38 years – 'Them Also Which Sleep in Jesus will God bring with him.' - Also the above Alexander Sloan, who died 16 April 1893, aged 40. - Also Peter, only son of the above, who lost his life with other brave officers in the Titanic Disaster, 15 April 1912, aged 31 years – 'Faithful unto Death.'

James Clinch Smith

Sailing and Equestrianism

Clinch Smith was born on 3 April 1856, at Smithtown in Suffolk County, on the north shore of Long Island, New York. He was the second son of three in a family of eleven children, born between 1846 and 1864, to Judge John Lawrence Smith (1816-1889), of Smithtown, and his wife Sarah Nicoll (formerly Clinch, 1823-1890), who was a niece of the owner of New York's first department store, A.T. Stewart. He was a descendant of the legendary Richard 'Bull Rider' Smith, the founder of Smithtown, and after whom the town was named.

He grew up on the family homestead in Smithtown and graduated from Columbia Law School in 1878. He practiced law as Smith and

Keene, with offices at 10 Wall Street in New York, and then in the Stewart Building at Broadway and Chambers Street.

He was a member of several New York elite clubs, including the Union Club with Archie Gracie, and became a popular figure in New York society, being one of 'Mrs Astor's Four Hundred'.

He was an accomplished sailor and rider, winning many prizes at the New York Horse Show. He was so keen on equestrianism, in fact, that he built his own racetrack, and was involved in organising the Smithtown Polo Club, gaining membership of the United States Polo Association.

In 1894 he was present at the Michaux Music Club in New York, where he met an accomplished Chicago musician and composer named Bertha Ludington Barnes. The couple married on 5 June 1895 at the Grace Church in Chicago, in a lavish wedding which was highly publicised and attended by all the well-known figures of Chicago society. They owned 'The Moorings', a beautiful villa overlooking the harbour in Newport. Apparently, their 'harvest dinner' in 1902, with its splendid farmyard decorations, was one of the highlights of the Newport social season.

In 1904 James and Bertha moved to Paris so that she could pursue her musical career and received much recognition for establishing her own all-female orchestra. James returned to New York at least once every year.

He was present at the rooftop theatre at Madison Square Garden in New York, watching the musical comedy *Mamzelle Champaign* being performed, when his brother-in-law, the architect Stanford White, was shot dead by Harry Kendall Thaw on 26 June 1906, and gave evidence at what became known as 'The Trial of the Century'. Thaw was acquitted by reason of insanity. Stanford White was married to his younger sister, Bessie Springs Smith.

By 1911 Bertha's obsession with music was causing strain in the marriage, and James went home to New York. However, in January

1912 Bertha asked him to come back to Paris to try to reconcile their marriage, and she agreed to give up her career and return to Smithtown with him. However, Bertha changed the plans at the last minute, and James decided to travel alone and get the homestead prepared for her return at a later date.

His body was never identified, but on 11 May 1912 a memorial service was held at St James' Episcopal Church, in the St James district of Smithtown, Long Island. Colonel Archibald Gracie was present, and he sat next to James' sister at the service, as his favourite hymn, 'Prayer for those at Sea', was sung. Colonel Gracie drew her attention to the fact that the same hymn had been sung at a service on *Titanic* on the morning before the disaster. It apparently had an effect on her, and she explained that the hymn had been the first piece set to music ever played by him as a child, 'and for which he was rewarded with a promised prize, donated by his father'.

Bertha died just over year later, officially of pneumonia, but many considered that the real cause of her death was a broken heart. There is a memorial stone dedicated to them both at St James' Church.

Charles Emil Henry Stengel
Horse Racing

Charles Stengel was born as Heinrich Stengel on 19 November 1857, at Newark in Essex County, New Jersey, United States. He was the oldest of three sons in a family of six children, born between 1855 and 1874, to German-born G. Jacob Stengel (1829-1898), and his New Yorker wife Mary Elizabeth (formerly Stumpf, 1835-1899). He was baptised at the First German Presbyterian Church in Newark, on 17 January 1858.

His father was a patent leather manufacturer who first arrived in America in 1846. In 1880 they lived at 02 Walnut Street in downtown Newark, and Charles had joined his father in the leather manufacturing business as a leather splitter. His father died in 1898, and his mother died in the following year, so Charles took over his father's business as a senior partner in the firm of Stengel and Rothschild.

In 1888 he married a New Yorker named Annie May Morris (1867-1956), and they had four children, all born in Newark: Jenny in 1888; Henry Ivan and Inez in 1892 (probably twins); and Karl Raymond (1895-1973). In 1900 the family were living at Spring Lake Borough in Monmouth, New Jersey, and a decade later they had returned to Newark, where they resided at 1075 Broad Street. Charles was described as being 5 feet 8 inches tall, with blue eyes and brown hair. He had a round face and chin, a high forehead and a regular nose.

The *Newark Evening News* for 17 April 1912, reported under the title 'First Direct Personal Message Received from Jersey Folk in the Disaster – Both on the Carpathia':

> Direct intelligence from Mr and Mrs C.E. Henry Stengel, of this city, now on the rescue ship *Carpathia*, was received here this afternoon by wireless. It was the first personal message from the Jersey folk who were on the *Titanic*, and came to Ivan Stengel at the leather factory of Stengel and Rothschild, at Maine and Kossuth Streets, at 1.30 o'clock. The message, which came by way of Halifax, reads as follows – 'Both on Carpathia. Have two automobiles to meet Carpathia. Have some survivors with us – Henry Stengel.' The last sentence has been taken to mean that Mr Stengel has offered some assistance to some of his fellow passengers on *Titanic*, who have been crippled by the disaster. Although the Stengels had been informed from the first that Mr and Mrs Stengel were among the rescued, the wireless brought much comfort and cheer.

It was later reported that the women Mr and Mrs Stengel had proposed to help could not be located when *Carpathia* docked in New York. He gave evidence at the United States inquiry on Day 11, 30 April.

A few weeks after the disaster, Charles Stengel was the victim of a racehorse scandal perpetrated by George Brereton, whose name appears on the *Titanic* passenger list as George Brayton. While he was on *Carpathia* he came across Brereton looking downcast, and when he was talking to him, he was surprised that Brereton knew his name. Brereton said that he had lost his money, and that he had no way of paying for the trip back to Los Angeles. Mr Stengel suggested that he should claim the cost of his fare from the White Star Line.

Not long after he reached home, Charles received a call from Brereton thanking him for his suggestion and telling him that the White Star Line had agreed to fund his passage home. However, Brereton said that he was not leaving for a while, so Charles invited him to his home for dinner. Zooming in on his interests in horse racing, Brereton put to Charles that his brother-in-law worked for the Western Union, and that they were planning a deal concerning horse racing which Charles might be interested in. The three men met at the Hotel Seville in New York, where it was put to Charles that Brereton's brother-in-law was able to delay the transmission of racing results so that they could back the winner before the result came through. Charles said that he did not want to get involved, and on telling the conmen what he thought, a scuffle broke out and the two men left before the police arrived.

On 19 April 1914, Charles Stengel became one of the first survivors to pass away, and the *New York Times* for 20 April 1914, reported:

> C.E. Henry Stengel, member of the firm of Stengel and Rothschild, manufacturer of leather, died yesterday at his home, 109 Lincoln Park in Newark, of pneumonia. He was one of the *Titanic* survivors. Mr Stengel was 56 years old, and was born in Newark. His father, G. Jacob Stengel, was one of Newark's pioneer leather manufacturers. Mr Stengel started in the leather business with Abraham Rothschild about 20 years ago. He is survived by a widow, a daughter, Mrs P.J. Horton; and two sons, Henry I and Carl Raymond Stengel.

His death certificate records his home address as 1075 Broad Street in Ward 2.

He was placed in the Stengel Mausoleum at Fairmount Cemetery in Newark. Annie died in 1956 and was placed in the mausoleum with her husband.

John Borland Thayer II
Cricket, Baseball and Lacrosse

John Thayer was born on 21 April 1862, at Haverford in Delaware County, Philadelphia, the second son of five in the Brahmin family of six children, born between 1860 and 1875, to John Borland Thayer (1836-1904), and his wife, Mary Randolph (formerly Chapman, 1839-1919). He was educated at the University of Pennsylvania in Philadelphia, where he was captain of the baseball team from 1879, and where he also played lacrosse.

The eleven-man team of cricket was introduced to Pennsylvania in the early eighteenth century by a group of men of English descent, who had played the game while students at the University of Pennsylvania. After graduating in 1854 they established the Philadelphia Cricket Club, which is one of the oldest in the United States, and is still active today. By the middle of the nineteenth century cricket was one of the most popular sports in the country, rivalling baseball, with notable clubs in Philadelphia, Pittsburgh and New York.

John became a member of the Merion Cricket Club at the age of 14, and his four brothers were noted cricketers who also played for the club. He played in seven cricket matches which are now recognised as first-class. Three for the 'Philadelphians', and four for 'American Born', all at the Germantown Cricket Club in Pennsylvania. His highest score was 24, and his best bowling averages were 3 for 17, both in the match for Pennsylvania against the United States in October 1883. In the summer of the same year, he toured England with a team of Philadelphia cricketers. During the tour he made 817 runs with an average of 28, his highest score being 93 versus Gentlemen of Derbyshire, and he took 22 wickets for 21 runs each.

James Lillywhite, the well-known Sussex cricketer and Test umpire, later said of him: 'For some years he was one of Philadelphia's leading cricketers. He bats in finished style, and, with more patience, would be the best in the team in that department. Can hit hard, and is a dangerous man when once well in. He bowls medium round arm, with good command of the ball and a break both ways. He is a splendid mid-off, and shows fine fielding whenever he is placed either at the boundary or close to the wicket.'

On leaving the University of Pennsylvania in 1881, John became a clerk in the offices of the Empire Line, part of the Pennsylvania Railroad. In 1888 he became freight solicitor for the United Railroads of New Jersey Division. From February 1889 he was not involved in railway work. However, from May 1892 he passed through all the grades of railway administration in the Eastern States. He returned to the Pennsylvania Railroad as freight agent of the Northern Central Division, with its main offices in Baltimore. By May 1899, the scope of his responsibilities as freight agent had widened to Northern Central, Philadelphia, Wilmington and Baltimore, and the West Jersey and Seashore Divisions. On 1 June 1903, he was elected fifth vice president of the Pennsylvania Railroad, achieving his main aim as second vice president on 2 March 1911.

On 9 November 1892 John married the daughter of a Philadelphia iron manufacturer named Marian Longstreth Morris, who was ten years his junior. They had four children, all born in Philadelphia: John Borland III, born in 1894; Frederick Morris, born in 1896; Margaret 'Peggy', born in 1898, and Pauline, born in 1901. The family lived in a large house named 'Redwood' at Lower Merion in Haverford.

He was a member of several prestigious clubs and organisations, including the Philadelphia Club, the Metropolitan Club of Washington DC, the Union League and the Union Club of New York, The Railroad Club of New York, and the Chamber of Commerce of the State of New York.

The Board of Directors of the Pennsylvania Railroad stated in the *Railway Age Gazette* for 26 April 1912:

> In recording the terrible fate of a valued officer, and beloved and respected associate, we desire to pay fitting tribute to his memory

> and bear testimony to his great worth to the company, not only as an officer, but in its highest councils.
>
> Mr Thayer was thoroughly equipped for the high office which he held, by his long service in the traffic department of the company, having discharged the duties of various official positions with the same diligence, intelligence and skill which were manifested and more highly developed in his executive life, until, through the channels of work well done and achievements of lasting importance, his name finds place on the roll of honour of those who have served the company faithfully and well: while to those who laboured side by side with him his memory, though darkened by the tragic ending of his life at the high tide of his usefulness, is made more dear by the characteristic manhood and heroism with which he accepted his fate.
>
> His true value to the company did not consist alone in his ability as an executive officer and prominent standing as a traffic authority; his alert mind and power of ready expression made for much in argument, debate and negotiation, and never were the interests of the company safer than in his hands. A man in all that endears men to men, of genial nature, with an affable manner and a ready appreciation of humour, he was a charming companion and beloved by all who knew him, while the example of his integrity, honourable dealing and clean life is an inspiration alike to friends, associates and subordinates.

Most of his direct family are buried at the Church of the Redeemer Cemetery at Bryn Mawr, Montgomery County, Pennsylvania, and there is a memorial dedicated to him inside the church. In 1920 Marian lived in the house on the Thayer Estate at Latches Lane in Merion. For a while after the disaster, Bruce Ismay corresponded with her, admitting, 'You had a very peculiar attraction to me.' Ten of the letters are preserved in the John B. Thayer Memorial Collection, held at the University of Pennsylvania's Kislak Center for Special Collections, which is an archive of first-hand accounts and other material, created by his wife Marian, and his son Jack.

John Borland 'Jack' Thayer III

Cricket, Figure Skating, Golf, Racquets and Hunting

Jack Thayer III was born on 24 December 1894, at Haverford in Philadelphia. He was the oldest child of John Borland Thayer II and his wife Marian.

In August 1914, with war clouds looming, he sailed to England from New York on RMS *Oceanic*, to play cricket in and around London for a Merion Cricket Club team from Haverford in Pennsylvania. In 1916 he was playing for the University of Pennsylvania Soccer team.

While on board *Oceanic* he met Officer Charles Lightoller who was working on the vessel. 'We again went over our experiences and checked our ideas of just what had happened. We agreed on almost everything, with the exception of the splitting or bending of the ship. He did not think it broke at all.'

Jack was an honorary member of the First Troop of Philadelphia City Cavalry, which had taken part in the battle of Gettysburg in 1865, and is still in existence today as part of the Pennsylvanian Army National Guard. When America was brought into the First World War in 1917, he was commissioned as captain of Artillery in the 79th Division, American Expeditionary Force. The division was organised at Camp Meade in Maryland, in August 1917, from men of Maryland, Pennsylvania and the District of Columbia, and sailed to Europe in July 1918. It saw extensive combat in the Meuse-Argonne Offensive area, fighting from 26 September to11 November 1918, where it earned the name of 'Cross of Lorraine' for the defence of France.

On 15 December 1917 Jack married Lois Buchanan Cassatt (1894-1977). Her grandfather had been a president of the Philadelphia Railway, which is probably why they got together. They had six children, all born in Haverford: John Borland IV was born in 1918; Alexander in 1920 (he died as an infant in the same year); Edward in 1921; Lois in 1923; Julie 'Dody' in 1928, and Pauline 'Polly' in 1930.

In October 1943 Second Lieutenant Edward Thayer, a bomber pilot with the United States Air Force, was shot down over Gargreave Island in the south-west Pacific Ocean area, and his body was never recovered. His mother died on 14 April 1944, which was the 32nd anniversary of the death of his father. These tragedies seemed to have sent Jack into a depression.

On 20 September 1945, Jack took his own life in a car parked at the junction of 48th Street and Parkside Avenue in Philadelphia, aged 50. He was buried at the Church of the Redeemer Cemetery at Bryn Mawr, Montgomery County in Pennsylvania, where most of his family were also laid to rest.

His detailed obituary in the *Philadelphia Inquirer* for 23 September 1945, read:

> John B. Thayer III, financial vice-president of the University of Pennsylvania, and a member of an old Philadelphia family, who had been reported missing since Wednesday, was found dead, his wrists and throat cut, in a parked automobile near the P.T.C. loop at 48th Street and Parkside Avenue yesterday morning.
>
> Coroner J. Allan Bertolet, one of the first to arrive on the scene after the body was discovered by two P.T.C. employees, said Mr Thayer probably had died forty hours before the body was found at 8:50 am. The coroner, who was accompanied by his chief deputy, Matthew A. Roth, said he believed that the death was a suicide.
>
> Frederick M. Thayer, a brother, of Newtown Square, and Lieutenant Governor John C. Bell, Junior, a lifelong friend, identified the body at the morgue.
>
> Mr Bell said that Mr Thayer had been suffering from a nervous breakdown during the last two weeks. 'The breakdown,' Mr Bell explained, 'was due, I believe, to worrying about the death of his son, Edward C. Thayer, who was killed in the service.'
>
> Mr Bell said that he reported Mr Thayer missing to the State Police, when the latter failed to return to his home in Grays Lane, Haverford, on Tuesday night.
>
> The Lieutenant governor stated that a few days ago Mr Thayer had, 'seemed to develop amnesia.' Mr Bell added that Mr Thayer had not been seen since he left his office in the University of Pennsylvania on Tuesday morning.
>
> The son, one of two who went to war, was Second Lieutenant Edward C. Thayer, a co-pilot of an army bomber, who was killed in action in the Pacific last October, the first member of the First City Troop to die in the Second World War. The other son, John B. Thayer IV, is a lieutenant and a Naval Air Force pilot.
>
> The P.T.C. employees who found the body on the front seat of the car with the feet under the steering wheel are George E. Wharton, of 2036 North 54th Street, a supervisor, and Daniel Petetti, a mechanic, of 1247 North 54th Street.

They said they first saw the automobile, a sedan, registered in the name of his wife, Mrs Lois C. Thayer, parked adjacent to the trolley loop on the south side of Parkside Avenue at noon on Thursday. When they saw the same car parked there yesterday, they investigated. The auto with Mr Thayer's body in it had gone unnoticed by trolley car passengers and boys who played football nearby.

The P.T.C. men, after finding the body, telephoned police. Patrolmen John Berry and Johjn Joynes, of the 50th Street and Lancaster Avenue station, took the body to the Presbyterian Hospital.

Deputy Coroner Roth, after the body was identified, said that there was no doubt that Mr Thayer used razor blades, which the police found in the car, to kill himself.

Doctor Thomas S. Gates, chairman of the University of Pennsylvania, in a formal statement, declared, 'In the death of Mr John B. Thayer, trustee, financial vice-president and former treasurer, the University of Pennsylvania has lost a trusted and loyal servant. He has given unsparingly of himself to his university and to community affairs, and he had redoubled his efforts in the war period, especially after the death of his son, Edward in the Pacific, which was followed closely by the death of his mother.'

Mr Thayer's mother, Mrs Marian Longstreth Morris Thayer, died at her Haverford home on 14 April 1944, which was the thirty-second anniversary of her husband's death on the liner *Titanic*, which sank after striking an iceberg in the Atlantic. Mrs Thayer and a younger son, Frederick, had been placed in a lifeboat, while John stood with his father on the *Titanic*'s deck when the ship went down. The younger Thayer was rescued. [This statement was later corrected].

Mr Thayer, who was 50, came from a family which had long been active in the affairs of the University of Pennsylvania. In 1928 he was elected trustee, and on 2 October 1939, he became treasurer of the university. In February 1944, he was appointed to the newly-created office of financial vice-president. He also was a director of the bi-centennial celebration of the University of Pennsylvania in 1940.

A graduate of the College of Arts and Sciences at the university, Mr Thayer was active in athletics and on undergraduate publications, and was a member of the Phi Beta Junior Society, Sphinx Senior Society and the Delta Psi Fraternity.

During the First World War he served as a captain in the Artillery of the 79th Division, and was an honorary member of the First Troop of Philadelphia Cavalry. In 1919 Mr Thayer entered the employ of Lee,

> Higginson and Company, bankers, in charge of their Philadelphia office. He left the firm in 1932 to become a partner in Yarnall and Company, from which he resigned in 1937.
>
> He also served as a member of the managing committee of the university, as a member of the General Alumni Society Board of Directors, and as chairman of the Alumni Annual Giving Fund Committee.
>
> He also was a director of the Academy of Fine Arts and chairman of the board of trustees of the Haverford School, of which he was a graduate. He was president of the Philadelphia Skating Club and Humane Society, and his hobby was figure skating.
>
> Mr Thayer was president of the Racquet Club, and former president of the Bond Club of Philadelphia. He was a member of the Rose Tree Fox Hunt, the Gulph Mills Golf Club. His father was a vice-president of the Pennsylvania Railroad, and was a member of the class of 1882 at the University of Pennsylvania.
>
> Mrs Thayer, who was the former Lois B. Cassatt, is a granddaughter of the late Alexander J. Cssatt, former president of the Philadelphia Railroad. Her parents were Colonel and Mrs Edward B. Cassatt. Colonel Cassatt, a graduate of West Point, served throughout the Spanish-American War, Philippine Campaign, and the First World War.

In 1940 Jack had his recollections of the *Titanic* disaster printed in 500 booklets to give out to his family and friends. For just over seven decades, the copies became mislaid or even discarded, until one was discovered at the time of the centenary by Lorin Stein, who was the editor of the literary magazine *Paris Review*, and a relative of the Thayer family. The copy was inscribed to his great-grandfather. It was published in 2012 with the title: *A Survivor's Tale: The Sinking of Titanic, 1912-2012*. Ironically, the book launch took place at the St Regis Hotel in New York, which had been built by *Titanic* victim John Jacob Astor.

Isaac George 'James' Widgery
Swimming and Bowling

Isaac (known as James) Widgery was born on 21 March 1875, in the Clifton district of Bristol. He was the eldest of a family of three boys and a girl to William Henry Widgery, a provisions merchant from Willand in Devon, and his wife Jessie (formerly Hoare), who had married in Somerset in 1870. His mother had been born to British parents in the Punjab, India.

The 1881 census records the family living at 1 Stanley Terrace, Bath Road, in the district of Bedminster, Bristol, and a decade later they lived at 127 Coronation Road in Bedminster. By 1901 he and his father lived at 11 Oakfield Road in Bristol, and he is described as a Hindu clothing manufacturer; possibly a skill he had picked up from his mother. When he was not at sea he lived with his brother Francis at 25 Rokeby Avenue, in the Redland district of Bristol.

On 17 September 1906, James arrived in the United States on board SS *New York*, and on 8 December 1909, he, seemingly unsuccessfully, petitioned for United States citizenship. He gave his temporary address as SS *New York*, Prier 14, New York City. He was described as a steward, was 5 feet 10 inches tall, with brown hair, blue eyes, and a dark complexion. He would meet the SS *New York* again in Southampton Harbour on 10 April 1912, when she nearly collided with *Titanic* and put a stop to her maiden voyage.

When he signed on to *Titanic*, his previous ship had been *St Paul*, and he gave his address as 67 Oxford Street in Southampton, which was a lodging address for seamen.

After the sinking he was called to give evidence at the United States Senate Inquiry on Day 7, 25 April 1912.

On 27 August 1913, at St Paul's Church in Clifton, Bristol, he married a young Bristol widow named Ann Elizabeth Callender (formerly Cooper), and they had daughters named Margaret Elizabeth (born in 1915) and Cynthia Mary (born in 1922). They lived at 31 Linden Road in Redland, where he was a member of the St Nicholas Lodge of Freemasons, and the Arrow Bowling Club.

James worked as an accountant and provisions merchant, a job which seems to have taken him across the sea many times, to places like Las Palmas and Tenerife in the Canary Islands. He always travelled alone on ships of the Yeoward Line.

James died on 21 August 1942, aged 67, in the Redland district of Bristol, and he was buried with his parents at St Andrew's churchyard in the village of Chew Magna near Bath. The grave inscriptions read:

In Loving Memory of William Henry Widgery
Of Bristol and Chew Magna,
Who Died March 1st 1930, aged 78 years.
Also of Jessie, Wife of the Above
Who Died February 4th 1937, Aged 83 years.
Also of Isaac George Widgery
Who Died August 21st 1942, aged 67
Beloved Husband of Anne Elizabeth
His Dearly Beloved Wife
Who Died February 6th 1962, Aged 84.
Also of Their Daughter Margaret
Who Died November 4th 2003, Aged 88 Years.

Charles Eugene Williams
Squash Racquets

Charles Williams was born on 28 July 1888, at Brompton in west London. He was the elder of two sons in a family of four children, born in west London between 1882 and 1893, to a Welshman named Edmund Williams, and his French-born wife, who was of Welsh parentage, named Elizabeth (formerly Holland). They both worked as tailors. At the time of the 1901 census, they were living at 5 Cottage Place in Westminster, London. Charles showed good aptitude with a racket from a young age, becoming a ball boy at London's socially exclusive gentlemen's Prince's Club in Knightsbridge.

It appears that the game of squash racquets was first played in London prisons as early as 1759, before it became established in London pubs. Harrow was the first school at which it was played, probably as early as 1820, when the schoolyard was enlarged, and the first covered squash court was built in 1865. It is still in use today. The early world championships were played for at irregular dates, and at the Olympic Games of 1908 all seven competitors were classed as British, although John Jacob Astor V was born in New York (see Sporting Connections).

On 6 August 1911, James married a Chelsea girl named Lois Wilkins. On 29 March 1912, they celebrated the birth of Eugene Charles, by which time the census recorded the family living at 2 Drury Road in Harrow, and Charles was described as a racquet professional at Harrow School, where he held the position of games master.

In January 1911 Charles beat Edgar Maximilian Baerlien to win the racquets open championship of England, and a few months later he was the challenger for the world championship against Jamsetji Merwanji of India, who had won the title in 1903. Charles won all four matches played at the Queen's Club, and played out a 3-3 draw in the second round at the Prince's Club, with the last match not being completed, to become the world champion at the age of 22.

In the following year the championships were to be played in New York on 29 April. Charles was to defend his title for a stake of $5,000 against the American champion, George Standing. However, the match was postponed.

After the disaster he sent a telegram to the honourable secretary of the Racquets Association, which read, 'Match postponed, return next week, Williams.' While he was in New York and still suffering from a great reduction in his strength and an injured arm and hand, he was also diagnosed with pneumonia, from which he would never fully recover. He admitted himself to a sanatorium to recuperate until he returned home to his family in Harrow a couple of weeks later.

Harrow School was visited by King George V and Queen Mary in June 1912, and Charles had a private audience with the royal couple in which he discussed his experience of the disaster.

For the 1913 championship he played Jock Soutar of the United States. Having won four of the six matches played at the Queen's Club, he lost all four matches played at the Philadelphia Club and therefore lost the title. He challenged Soutar again in 1922, but lost four of the seven games played at the Philadelphia Club and the New York Club.

He and Lois remained in Harrow and went on to have another five children, a boy and four girls.

In 1924 he was offered a job as a professional at the newly opened Chicago Racquets Club. Charles and his family moved to America in July 1924 aboard *Titanic's* sister ship *Olympic*, and they settled at 5524 N Lakewood in Chicago, where Charles also worked as a tennis instructor.

He continued to train and compete with Jock Soutar, and in 1929 he challenged Soutar again for the world championship, and won 7-3 in matches played at the Philadelphia Club and the New York Club. He remained world champion for the rest of his life.

His descendants recall that he never talked about the *Titanic* disaster, but that he suffered from many infections as his lungs never fully recovered after catching pneumonia in New York. Charles contracted bronchial pneumonia and after just a week he suddenly passed away on 27 October 1935, aged just 47, and was buried at the Rosehill Cemetery in Chicago. His descendants still own a spoon he is said to have carried off the ship.

Leslie Williams
Boxing

Leslie Williams was born at Tonypandy in Glamorgan, south Wales, during the summer of 1888. He was the fourth and youngest son of eight surviving children, born between 1875 and 1891, to Albert Clive Williams, who had been born at Kidsgrove in Stoke-on-Trent in 1865, and his wife, Mary Jane (formerly Thomas), who had been born at Ebbw Vale in 1866.

Leslie first appears on the 1891 census, when the family was living at 4 Fearnley Terrace in Clydach, Ystradyfodwg, in the Rhondda Valley, and a decade later they had moved to 19 Gleaner Street. Although Leslie was only 12 years old, he had left school and was working as an apprentice boilermaker.

In 1910 he married Lily Thomas (born at Tonypandy on 1 July 1891), and a son named Leslie James was born to them on 29 October 1910. In 1911 they lived at 59 Primrose Street in Tonypandy. When Leslie left for Southampton, Lillie was pregnant with their second child.

Leslie began working as a blacksmith, but had decided to take up boxing as a profession, and his ring weight was 8 stone 10 pounds or bantamweight. He had fought in twelve bouts between March 1908 and December 1911, winning six, all on points, and losing two, being knocked-out in his last fight. He had also drawn one, had a no contest decision, and was disqualified in another. He too had fought several bouts at the Millfield Athletic Club, and he had also fought twice in Paris. His full record was:

30 March 1908 – lost on points to Fred Young Delaney at Millfield Air Corps in Pontypridd

14 December 1908 – beat Dai Stephens on points at Ynsanghared Hall in Pontypridd

30 August 1909 – no contest against Phineas Emmanuel at Millfield Air Corps in Pontypridd

28 January 1910 – drew with Fernand Cuny at Elysee Montmarte in Paris

1 April 1910 – beat Young Warner on points at Elysee Montmartre in Paris

4 July 1910 – beat Ike Young Bradley on points at Millfield Air Corps in Pontypridd

31 October 1910 – lost to Munroe Grainger on points at Millfield Air Corps in Pontypridd

17 December 1910 – lost to Georges Bernard on points at Wonderland in Paris

13 February 1911 – beat Young Johnny Walters on points at Millfield Air Corps in Pontypridd

17 April 1911 – beat Young Warner on points at Millfield Air Corps in Pontypridd

8 May 1911 – beat Tickler Lunt on points at Olympia in Edinburgh

9 December 1911 – lost by knock out to Arthur Evans at Pavilion Rink in Bargoed

On 5 March 1912, he took part in the Nazareth House tournament at the Park Hall in Cardiff, where he impressed Jim Driscoll with his performance against Joe Bowker, the former world champion.

Leslie was body number fourteen picked up by the *Mackay-Bennett* on 22 April 1912. He was identified by his effects. He was wearing a green overcoat over a blue serge suit, with a red striped shirt and two scarves. He had on his person two gold rings, a pair of silver cuff links, a knife, two pocketbooks, papers, a ticket, and an amount of money in dollar gold, pounds and pennies. His possessions were returned to his wife, who wanted his remains to be brought back to Wales for burial, but unfortunately his body was buried at sea. Two pennies from the year 1899 and 1900 were retrieved by the family as treasured mementoes. A benefit to help the families was held at the Mid-Rhondda Athletic Grounds on 22 April 1912, consisting of a gymkhana and assault-at-arms tournament, and numerous well-known boxers supported the cause.

Lily gave birth to a son named Harold Charles on 25 July 1912. According to family history, a local coal miner named Dan Winter had promised that if anything should happen to Leslie, he would look after Lillie. He kept to his word and they married in 1914, having several more children.

Charles Duane Williams
Lawn Tennis

Charles Williams, usually known as Duane, was born on 11 August 1860, in Radnor, Delaware County, Pennsylvania. He was the son of Duane Williams, a direct descendant of the American statesman Benjamin Franklin, and his wife Alice (formerly Norris), who had married in Philadelphia on 8 October 1857. He had a brother named Richard Norris who was two years older. Their mother died on 10 February 1863, aged 27, and their father died in Philadelphia on 4 August 1863, aged 31, leaving them as orphans.

Duane worked as an attorney, and he and Richard were on board the British passenger liner SS *Arizona* on its way from New York to Liverpool when it smashed head-on into an iceberg in the North Atlantic on 7 November 1879. Fortunately, the vessel managed to stay afloat and get to St John's to receive temporary repairs to its badly damaged bow, before being taken on the vessel the *Glasgow*.

On 8 April 1884, he married Lydia Biddle (formerly White, 1864-1946). Lydia was of an old Philadelphia family. They were originally Quakers who had sailed to America from England to escape religious persecution.

Duane and his son, Richard, were travelling on the *Titanic* to Radnor in Pennsylvania, where Lydia lived.

Le Journal de Genève for 25 April 1912, published the following letter in French, which had been received from a Mr Wm J. M:

> It was with deep sorrow that we learnt in Geneva that Mr C. Duane Williams was among the victims of the *Titanic*.
>
> Indeed, Mr Williams only had friends in this city. He was a citizen of the great republic of North America; he passionately loved Geneva, so much in fact that he came here for two days only and in fact spent nineteen years of his life.
>
> His frankness and warmth turned everyone around him into friends, and he was also a tactful and generous man to a rare level. He was a man who never was indifferent to anybody's trouble or misery. This is a detail that will tell you a lot about him; he complained that he did not pay enough taxes in a city where he felt at home.
>
> His son was the tennis champion Richard N. Williams. Mr Williams senior promoted this sport in this country, and no one can deny that it is thanks to him that tennis wonderfully spread in Geneva in the last years.
>
> Those who had the privilege to know this man of good, will never forget this nice character, his sparkling eyes full of bounty, the way

> this honest man frankly clutched your hands, the joyful, 'Hello my boys!' he welcomed us with. His death brings mourning to an ancient and respectable family from Philadelphia, and, at the same time, to many members of the Geneva family. To Mrs Williams, whose pain is only equal to her valour, to her son, miraculously saved from the disaster that made him an orphan, we send our moved sympathies, and we tell them that the souvenirs we keep of the dear dead dad will last forever.

His body was never identified, and a flask he carried on *Titanic* is still in the possession of the family.

Richard Norris Williams II
Lawn Tennis

Richard Norris Williams was born on 29 January 1891, in Geneva, Switzerland, the son of Charles and Lydia Williams. His early years were spent in Lausanne. He was educated privately at a Swiss boarding school and could speak fluent French and German.

He began playing lawn tennis at the age of 12, and under his father's guidance won the Swiss Junior Championships in 1911. He and his father were on their way from Europe to Radnor to visit his mother, after which he intended to enrol at Harvard University, and perhaps get the chance to play some tennis. He was a member of the California Golden Bears, a sports association based at the University of California in Berkeley.

After suffering hours in the icy waters of the Atlantic Ocean, he showed unbelievable resilience and determination to survive.

On 18 July 1912, at the venue of the Longwood Bowl Tournament played at the Longwood Cricket Club in Boston, he faced his fellow lawn tennis *Titanic* survivor, Karl Behr. After winning the first two sets, Behr took command of the match and Williams lost 6-0, 9-7, 2-6, 1-6, 4-6. However, he reached the finals of the Longwood Bowl Tournament three times, in 1919, 1921 and 1922, before winning the title in 1923. He gained revenge over Karl Behr in the final for the

Achilles Cup, played for during the Sea Bright Tournament in New Jersey.

A month later he won the United States mixed doubles title paired with Mary K. Browne in three sets. He entered Harvard University in 1912 and was Intercollegiate lawn tennis champion at singles in 1913 and 1915, and doubles in 1914 and 1915.

The *Adelaide Observer* for 6 November 1915, reported:

> R.N. Williams, the American national champion, by virtue of his victory over M.E, McLoughlin last year, retained the Achilles Cup at the Sea Bright tournament, New Jersey, USA, on 14 August. The challenger was Karl H. Behr, who to reach the last stage had put out McLoughlin.
>
> Williams won with scores of 7-6, 6-4, 3-6, 6-2. He brought off some beautiful passing-shots. Transversely, it was the worst thing that his challenger attempted to do. At no stage of the four sets did Behr display anything that approached the certainty and control of his drives that he had shown in his wonderful battle against McLoughlin. He was constantly driving into the net when he most needed points.
>
> Early in the contest Williams found that Behr was having trouble with his back hand. With the magnetic buoyancy of youth which the national champion always displays on the courts he went for that back hand with an intensity that was fairly tigerish. It brought its reward. At that time Behr had won the first four games of the opening set. He seemed to have things all his own way. Then the revolution set in. Gallantly the champion tried to gain the net to bring off his killing volleys. He was met by the smoothest passes that have been put across the nets this season.
>
> There was no checking Williams. Behr lobbed – it was poor lobbing at that – for the ball always fell short; Behr only offered Williams enticing opportunities for smashes which ended the rallies. Misfortune visited Behr at the most critical stage of' that eventful first set which marked the waning of his powers. He was fighting with all the fierce intensity to bring the games level when he broke his pet racket. Another smash, and the second weapon snapped, so that he had to borrow a racket to finish out part of the contest, using it until his best piece of armoury had been patched up.
>
> The impressive thing about the conflict was the ingenuity with which Williams worked his drives. He varied pace with the cunning of a magician. He caught Behr napping more than once and invariably

with the same result. The strange thing about it was that Williams hazarded everything on lightning shots just inside the lines, and in so doing be piled up plenty of errors. He made amends, however, by the brilliancy of his passes, by his winning shots, the shots that turned the tide in his favour.

The winner served 14 double faults. Yet his service proved a wonderfully managed weapon, although it amazed the crowd because of its many double faults. He sent the second ball across at the same terrific speed as the first. The method, a pet theory with Williams, proved its worth in the fact that he had 11 service aces to his credit, the majority of them scored at critical points in close games.

During the First World War in 1917, Richard sailed for active service with an artillery unit with the American Expeditionary Force, and served as a lieutenant and aide-de-camp to Major General John Harbord. For his service with the American Marine Corps at Belleau Wood during the second battle of the River Marne, 15 to 18 July 1918, he was awarded the French Croix de Guerre, and the Legion d'Honneur, the highest and most prestigious French national order of merit.

In Pennsylvania on 11 January 1919, Richard married a New York girl named Jean Haddock (1890-1929), and they lived at Newton in Middlesex County, Massachusetts. Jean died at Wayne in Delaware County, Pennsylvania, on 20 April 1929, aged 38.

Richard Norris Williams' Grand Slam Finals Record:

1912 – won United States mixed doubles title with Mary K Browne in three sets

1913 – lost United States singles title to Maurice McLoughlin in four sets

1914 – won United States singles title – beat Maurice McLoughlin in three sets

1916 – won United States singles title – beat William Johnston in five sets

1920 – won Wimbledon doubles championship with Chuck Garland in four sets

1921 – lost United States doubles title with Watson Washburn in three sets

1923 – lost United States doubles title with Watson Washburn in five sets

1924 – lost Wimbledon doubles final with Watson Washburn in five sets

1925 – won United States doubles title with Vincent Richards in four sets

1926 – won United States doubles title with Vincent Richards in four sets

1927 – lost United States doubles title with William Johnston in three sets

His record in the International Lawn Tennis Championships, known as the Davis Cup:

1913	United States 3 Great Britain 2 – won 1 lost 1 in singles
1914	Australasia 3 United States 2 – lost 2 singles
1921	United States 5 Japan 0 – won 1 doubles
1923	United States 4 Australasia 1 – won 1 doubles (long game)
1925	United States 5 France 0 – won 1 doubles
1926	United States 4 France 1 – won 1 doubles

United States Clay Court Championships:

1912	Won in three sets against the American, Walter T. Hayes.
1915	Won by default against the American, Clarence Griffin.

Both titles were won at Pittsburgh in Pennsylvania.

Pennsylvanian Lawn Tennis Championships, held at the Merion Cricket Club:

1912	Won in three 6-1 sets against Pittsburgh's Percy Dwight Siverd
1914	Won in four sets against Pennsylvanian Bill Tilden II
1915	Lost by walk over against the American Joseph J Armstrong
1925	Lost in five sets to the United States champion, Bill Tilden II
1927	Won in four sets against Manuel Alonso Areizaga of Spain

Having reached the 1924 Wimbledon semi-finals, where he lost to René Lacoste in four sets, he also lost the men's doubles final with Watson Washburn in four sets.

A few days later he took part in the 1924 Olympic Games in Paris, which was depicted in the motion picture *Chariots of Fire*. The matches were played at Stade Tennis de Colombes, just north of Paris. He lost to Henri Cochet of France in the quarter finals of the singles, and in the quarter finals of the men's doubles.

There were twenty-one pairs of players from fourteen countries in the mixed doubles championship, staged from14 to 21 July 1924, on which day he partnered Hazel Wightman, who later established the Wightman Cup. He played the match with a sprained ankle, but still went on to win the gold medal. The United States players won all five lawn tennis events. Lawn tennis events were not included in the Olympic Games from 1928 until the 2012 London Games, and so technically he remained an Olympic lawn tennis champion for eighty-four years.

He was a successful investment banker in Philadelphia, and was the president of the Historical Society of Pennsylvania, based in Philadelphia for twenty-two years.

On 2 October 1930, at the Church of Heavenly Rest in Manhattan, New York City, he married a New Yorker named Frances Sue West Gilmore (1908-2001), who was the only child of Major General Quincy Adams Gilmore (1881-1956). They had children named Duane Norris (1924-2010), and Frances Sue 'Susie' (1933-2009).

In 1957 he was inducted into the International Tennis Hall of Fame at the Newport Casino Complex on Rhode Island.

Richard died of emphysema on 2 June 1968, aged 77, at Bryn Mawr in Pennsylvania, and was buried at Old St David's Church Cemetery at Wayne in Delaware County, Pennsylvania.

Hugh Woolner

Rugby Union, Rowing and Athletics / Track and Field

Hugh Woolner was born on 28 September 1866, at 29 Welbeck Street in Marylebone, London, and was baptised at St Mary's Church in Marylebone. He was the second child and eldest of two sons in a family of six children, born between 1865 and 1874, to Thomas Woolner (1825-1892), a celebrated sculptor, poet and art collector, who exhibited his work at the Royal Academy, and his wife Alice Gertrude (formerly Waugh, 1845-1912). She was the youngest but one of eight daughters, and they had married in Kensington on 6 September 1864. In 1871 their address was Cavendish Square in Marylebone. His brother Geoffrey passed away from scarlet fever at the prestigious Marlborough College in Wiltshire, on 17 July 1882, aged 14.

Hugh was also educated at Marlborough College. There he played rugby union for Marlborough Nomads in a 'Grand football match' against Midland Counties. The Nomads were formed in 1868 by former pupils of Marlborough College who had moved to live and work in London, and their home matches were played at Surbiton. They were notable for being one of the founder members of the Rugby Football Union, and the club provided a number of international players.

He went up to Trinity College, Cambridge in 1885. Described as an imposing figure like his father, he was 6 feet 3 inches tall, his stature making him an ideal competitor in field events, and he gained a varsity blue for throwing the hammer against Oxford, reaching a distance of 93 feet and 10 inches (28.60 metres). He also represented Trinity College as a rower, and sometime during his career as a sportsman he received a blow below his left knee, which left a permanent scar.

On 17 September 1892 he married a Yorkshire girl named Mary Simpson (1868-1906), the daughter of a Scarborough vicar, at St Martin's-on-the-Hill in Scarborough. Their first child, Christopher Geoffrey, was born in 1893, followed by five girls born between

1895 and 1906. At the time of the 1901 census, they lived at Ford's Grove in Winchmore Hill near Enfield in north London. Mary died of a suspected brain aneurysm, aged only 38, at 127 Fellows Road in Hampstead, London, on 16 December 1906, only a few weeks after their daughter Christine had been born.

He had not been married long when his father suffered a stroke and died on 7 October1892, and soon afterwards he embarked on a career in finance. He began working at the London Stock Exchange and later established his own firm of Woolner and Company Brokers, with Nick Sumner-Jones. His mother died in London on 9 March 1912, not long before he sailed on *Titanic*, by which time he was a director of various companies. However, through some bad investments his company had been declared bankrupt in 1907.

He was called to testify at the United States Senate Inquiry on Day 10, 29 April 1912, and returned to Britain on the *Lusitania* on 4 June 1912.

On 13 August 1912 he married Mary 'Maisie' Aglaia Dowson (formerly Ionides), whose Turkish father was a fellow stockbroker and lived in Kensington. They had a son named Alexander Hugh 'Sandy', who was born in 1914. Hugh continued his business interests in London, residing at various addresses, including 815 Salisbury House.

His son Christopher Geoffrey, known as Kit Woolner, was commissioned into the Royal Engineers, and for gallantry on the Western Front during the First World War was awarded the Military Cross with two bars, and was three times mentioned in despatches. During the Second World War he was appointed Companion of the Order of the Bath (CB), and was twice mentioned in despatches. He rose to the rank of major general before his retirement in 1947.

The family address was 60 Crooms Hill in Greenwich, when Hugh and Mary went to Hungary to visit his cousin Percival Bentley Waugh, who was married to a Hungarian girl named Alrune Zsofia Antonia (formerly Koczy) and was living at Furj Utca 7a, a street just west of Budapest. While there he was stricken with pneumonia and died on 13 February 1935, aged 58. Mary died at Newton Abbot in Devon on Boxing Day, 1945.

Frederick Wright
Squash Racquets

Fred Wright was born on 3 December 1888, at Great Billing in Northamptonshire, and was baptised there on 6 January 1889. He was the youngest child of fifteen, born between 1866 and 1888, to a shoemaker named William Wright and his wife Esther (formerly Harlitt), who lived all their lives in Great Billing.

At the time of the 1891 census, he was living with his family at St Giles in Great Billing. However, his mother passed away in 1896, and his father, possibly finding it difficult to look after his large family, sent Fred to live with his older married brother William and his family at Alms House village, and on the 1901 census, at the age of 12, he is stated as having already started work as a domestic house boy. He does not appear on the 1911 census, but his father is recorded as living at St Giles in Great Billing, with his unmarried daughter Ida, and he was employed as an agricultural labourer.

When he signed on *Titanic*, Fred's address was at 67 Oxford Street in Southampton, and he also lived at 22 Stern Street in Shepherd's Bush, north London.

A series of letters he wrote to his sister while serving on board RMS *Olympic*, dated from 9 August 1911 to 13 March 1912, still exist. There are also a letter and a postcard he wrote while working on *Titanic*, which he described as 'The Best'.

The *Northampton Herald* of 24 May 1912, reported:

> Titanic Concert – At Great Billing on Sunday afternoon, a concert in the memory of the late Mr F Wright, who lost his life in the Titanic, was given by the Northampton Imperial Band, conducted by Mr S Piper, late of the 58th Regiment [Northamptonshire]. The band first

played two of the deceased's favourite hymns outside his father's house, and afterwards gave the following programme: March – 'To the Front' (J Hulme); selection - 'Sabbath Chimes' (H Round); cornet solo - 'Ora Pro Nobis (Piccolomini), Musician Walding; selection – 'Kyrie and Gloria' from Mozart's Twelfth Mass; hymn – 'Nearer My God, To Thee'; 'Funeral March')Chopin); hymn – 'Kyrie Eleeson *[sic]* (Mozart). The arrangements were made by Mr C.H. Ponting, and the following committee: Messrs F. Barber, A. Copson (treasurer), R. Britten, G. Clarke, and F. Bustin. A collection was taken for the Titanic Relief Fund.

Fred's name is included on the headstone of his mother's grave in St Andrews Churchyard in Great Billing, which reads:

In Loving Memory of Esther
The Dearly Beloved Wife of William Wright
Died August 27 1896, Aged 43 Years
Also of Frederick, Youngest son of above
Who was lost in the Founding
of SS Titanic on April 14 1912, Aged 24 Years.
Nearer Thy God to Thee.

His death inspired players in Philadelphia to hold a squash competition, which they named the Fred Wright Memorial Cup in his memory.

SPORTING CONNECTIONS

A member of the family of John Jacob Astor IV, who lost his life in the *Titanic* disaster, was John Jacob Astor V, his second cousin, who competed in the racquets championship at the 1908 London Olympic Games, taking bronze in the singles, and gold in the doubles. It was the only time the sport was included in the Games, meaning he is therefore still the reigning Olympic champion. He was also captain of the Royal Cinque Ports Golf Club, president of the Hurlingham Club, and in 1937 became the president of the MCC.

The Vanderbilt family was among the richest in the United States, and a member of the family established the Vanderbilt Cup in 1904, the first motor sports race in the United States. Alfred Gwynn Vanderbilt was a keen sportsman, who participated in coaching and hunting, and twenty-seven of his horses competed at the International Horse Show held at Olympia in London in June 1907. He died in the sinking of the *Lusitania* in 1915, and some of his coaching friends erected a memorial to him at the side of the A24 London to Worthing Road near Dorking, on what is said to have been his favourite road.

His cousin was George Washington Vanderbilt, and according to the *New York Tribune* for 30 April 1912, he had a close call concerning the *Titanic*. It reported:

> Mr and Mrs George W. Vanderbilt escaped death or the hazard of life on the *Titanic* because they heeded the request of Mrs [Edith] Vanderbilt's mother, Mrs Dresser, not to sail on any ship making its first voyage.

> The Vanderbilt's had engaged rooms on *Titanic*, and had sent part of their baggage on board in charge of their footman Edwin Charles Wheeler, known as Frederick. When Mrs Dresser was informed of their plans, she declared that an untried ship was dangerous, and was so insistent that the Vanderbilt's cancelled their booking and came under another ship. Wheeler remained on *Titanic* and was lost.

The Vanderbilts travelled home on RMS *Olympic*, which arrived in New York on the day *Titanic* set sail. Edith Dresser's mother Susan had died in 1883, and it was her much-travelled oldest sister, also named Susan, who had talked them out of sailing on the doomed ship.

Among the third-class passengers was Rhoda Abbott, who was travelling with her two teenage sons, Rossmore and Eugene. She had been married to the London-born ex-United States Middleweight Boxing Champion, Stanton Abbott.

They had been asleep when a steward alerted them of the danger, and they put on lifejackets and went up to the second-class saloon area. Rossmore is said to have dropped to his knees and prayed that his mother might be saved, even if he and his brother were not. All three were allowed to approach emergency lifeboat C, but when Rhoda realised that her sons were not being allowed to board the craft with her, she stepped back.

As the ship sank and the sea engulfed the deck, the Abbotts were swept overboard. Rhoda tried to clasp hold of her sons but to no avail. She swam around in the freezing water for some time trying to find them, but then she saw collapsible A and struggled to get on board. Rhoda is believed to have been the only woman who went in the water and survived. Her legs were badly injured, but she was glad she remained on *Titanic* until the last because it allowed her to remain with her sons. Rossmore's body was later recovered, but Eugene's was not.

NEWSPAPER REPORTS AND INQUIRIES

Under the title 'Graphic Stories of the Passengers', The *Sydney Truth* for 21 April 1912, reported on the disaster:

Thousands of people were waiting on the wharf for the arrival of the *Carpathia,* which has the survivors of the *Titanic* wreck on board. The excitement was intense, and pitiful scenes were witnessed as the relatives of those who were on board the gigantic liner took their place on the dock, eagerly awaiting the arrival of the vessel which may and may not have their dear ones on board.

As the liner came in towards the dock the people on the wharf nearly went crazy with excitement. The relatives were arranged on the dock in alphabetical order, so that the work of determining whether their relatives were rescued or not would be facilitated. The *Carpathia*'s decks were jammed with a surging mass of people, who waved their hats and hands to those on shore. It was an impressive scene, for the surging mass on the dock stood with silent lips and bowed and uncovered heads as the passengers hurried off and the ambulance men hurried to and fro with instruments and surgical help for those on board who needed them.

Mrs Andrews, one of the rescued passengers, said that the crash came at 11.35, and she and others were off in a lifeboat by 12.15. The *Titanic* plunged to the bottom at 2 am. She and her party were six and a half hours in an open boat, suffering terribly from the icy blasts and the terror of the situation, before the *Carpathia* was sighted. 'We never saw the *Carpathia,*' she said, 'until daybreak.' When the

Titanic struck the berg the water rushed in, and the boat began to sink at the bow. Alarms were given, and the passengers seized whatever clothes were nearest. 'Immediately the boats were made ready we heard some shooting amongst the first-class passengers. The ship's band, when the first crash occurred, assembled in the stern and played the hymn, "Nearer My God to Thee," as the boat went down.'

Others describe the scene as the most awfully impressive it is possible to imagine. When the vessel plunged into the depths most of the lifeboats were far away, and across the dark waters were wafted the strains of the hymn. Then there was a terrific noise, and the music ceased. The ship had plunged two miles to the bottom.

The wireless operator refused to desert his post but was torn away by a party who feared that he was erased. A despicable action followed. A number of first-class passengers attacked him in order to secure the lifebelt that had been placed upon him. A fight in the wireless cabin followed amongst those who were endeavouring to secure the precious belt that had been taken from the wireless operator, but what the melee resulted in the survivors are unable to tell.

It is said that the captain was washed off the bridge, but that he swam back to the vessel, and sank with her. The Associated Press says that Lord and Lady Duff-Gordon were saved.

Colonel Gracie says that before retiring to his cabin he was chatting with Mr Hays, president of the Canadian Grand Trunk Railway, who said that the Cunard, White Star, and Hamburg- American steamship lines, were devoting their attention and ingenuity to the attainment of supremacy in the direction of luxury and speed. 'The time will come,' said Hay, 'when this will be capped by some appalling disaster.'

Mr Hugh Woolner, a rich Londoner and a Cambridge oarsman, says, 'The shock of the impact was so slight that we were not thrown from our chairs. For half an hour we, walked the deck, not realising our danger. I helped to load the boats afterwards. Several foreigners attempted to jump into them ahead of the women. An officer fired two shots into the air to restrain them, and a friend and I jumped into the boats and pulled the men out. I was picked up by a boat that was not full, and helped to row. We saw the ship sink with the lights burning. She was at an angle of 45 degrees. On this account there was very little suction. It seemed an eternity before the *Carpathia* arrived.'

It is stated that Captain Smith, when he was washed from the bridge, swam to pick up a baby, which was struggling in the water and drowning. He took the little mite to a lifeboat and then heroically swam hack to his sinking ship.

A London passenger states that thirty men were on board one of the collapsible rafts, which slowly sank until they were up to their waists in water. After a few hours, however, it slowly righted itself. A waiter on the *Titanic* said that the iceberg looked like a gigantic mountain of glass. When he heard the stokehold was filling with water he knew that there was no hope. The officers called for volunteers to go below and draw the fires, and twenty men responded to the call.

A thrilling story was told by an Irish girl, one of the steerage passengers. She said that she saw four steerage passengers (men) jump into a lifeboat. An officer jumped forward and shot the four of them. The bodies were thrown into the ocean. Time and again the officers dragged men out of the boats to make way for the women. One child had the scarlet fever, and another had meningitis. An epidemic of measles had broken out on board during the voyage.

One version of the deaths of Colonel Astor and Mr Stead, the famous journalist, is told by Mr Phillip Mock. He said that the two men clung to a raft until their feet were frozen. They were then compelled to release their hold, and, dropping back into the frigid waters, they quietly slipped through the threshold of death.

According to the story told by a surgeon who boarded the *Carpathia* after she was docked, four bodies were buried at sea. The chief steward explained that a large number of the crew were saved. The majority of them jumped into the water, and were picked up by the lifeboats afterwards.

Henry Harris, the well-known theatrical manager, tried to reach a boat with his wife, but the second officer held him back with a gun, and threatened to blow his brains out if he proceeded until the women were placed into the lifeboats. A third-class passenger attempted to climb into a boat before the women and children had been placed therein, and he was immediately shot by a steward. Another passenger says that a lady named Mrs Straus asked an officer whether her husband would be allowed to accompany her in the lifeboat. She was told that he could not, and she stepped out of the boat, and remained with her husband, going to her death at his side.

Edward Wheelton, chief steward of the *Titanic*, says: 'Sunday night was quite clear, although a light fog had commenced to rise. Many of the passengers were on deck and in the saloons, dancing and having music. Suddenly there was a crash amidships, but there was no immediate commotion, for the passengers did not realise the extent of the damage. They were reassured by the officers, who themselves for the moment did not realise that the ship had received her death blow. Then the vessel commenced to fill and sink at the head, and the officers came to the conclusion, that it was advisable to lower the boats. The women and children were placed in the lifeboats, and the men bade them goodbye just as if they were separating for a short time. I heard Colonel Astor tell his wife that they would meet in New York. I saw President Taft's aide-de-camp, Major Butt, control the men who were inclined to get into a panic, and give orders in a calm voice. During the excitement the band assembled, and played operatic selections in order to allay the passengers' ears. Later on, when it was plain that the vessel must sink, and that hundreds of them would go down with her, the band played the hymn, 'Nearer My God to Thee.' Then the boats pushed away, and two hours afterwards we suddenly saw the Titanic lurch upward and sink.'

Mr Bruce Ismay, managing director of the firm of Ismay, Imrie, and Co., owners of the White Star Line, in an interview, said, 'During the present state of affairs I feel too deeply for expression. I say, however, that the White Star officers did everything possible to alleviate the suffering and the sorrows of the relatives and friends of those who perished. After striking, the vessel remained two hours and 25 minutes above water before taking her final plunge.'

Quartermaster Moody says that the first officer, who was on the bridge at the time, shot himself when he realised the seriousness of the position. 'We were running at about 23 miles an hour,' said Moody, 'and encountered a cloudy haze, which prevented us seeing more than two lengths ahead. When we struck there was no chance of closing the compartment doors. During the day we made 565 miles.'

Mr C.E. Stengel, a well-known New York racehorse owner, says that the upsetting of a lifeboat when it was being lowered into the water cost the lives of Lord Duff Gordon and Lady Gordon. Official figures place the number of saved at 705.

Later, in the course of a further interview, Mr Ismay, whose action in leaving the vessel so early has been adversely commented upon, claims that the accident was not due to any carelessness and says that it was an act of God. He defends his action in taking a lifeboat and says that the one he got into was the last to leave the doomed ship. Asked whether there were any women and children on board when he got into the boat, he replied, 'couldn't say.'

Dr Washington Dodge said: 'Major Butt and Colonel Astor stood on the bridge with their arms entwined. I am confident that the *Titanic* broke in two. All the boats were not filled, since the passengers believed that it was impossible for the ship to sink. When the lifeboats were leaving the ship, many of the passengers on board stood at the rails and ridiculed those in the boats, saying that they were foolish to go into the lifeboats, because it was impossible for the *Titanic* to sink. They called them landlubbers, and jeered at them. They were soon disillusioned, however, for the ship sank lower and lower, and when the water reached the top decks of the first-class those on board realised that the position was indeed a serious one.'

Other survivors relate stories of the wreck. It seems that uncontrollable terror seized many of the passengers when the vessel struck. They frantically endeavoured to tear up the deck fittings for the purpose of making rafts, because they realised that there would not be sufficient boats for all. Some of them jumped overboard, and a few were saved. Some say that there were two separate explosions, which blew the bowels out of the vessel, while others declare that they heard no explosions. No eye-witness can be found to corroborate the story that some of the men who rushed the boats before the women and children were placed therein were shot by the officers. It is positively asserted that the captain did not commit suicide. Many women attempted to jump overboard, but they were forcibly restrained. Children old enough to realise the seriousness of the position did much to cheer their parents. They are the real heroes.

Dealing with the accident, Mr Ismay says, 'The whole bilge was ripped out where the iceberg caught the vessel a glancing blow on the starboard side. The vessel seemed to climb up on the submerged part of the berg. The watertight compartments were not saved, because the plates on the starboard quarter were loosened, and the forward compartments flooded. I sent a statement of the wreck to the White Star offices by wireless on Monday morning at 10.' It is asserted, however, that this statement was not received until Wednesday. Many sailors who might have saved themselves deliberately stood aside to let the women take their places in the boat.

Miss Slater says that nobody is deserving of more credit than the ship's orchestra. 'We were ordered back to bed,' she said, 'and in half an hour there was a general order to don lifebelts given. The deck presented an indescribable sight a number of the steerage men attempting to seize the lifeboats. They were beaten back by the officers, and a brisk revolver fire followed, as a result of which many fell. The prompt action of the officers did a lot to restore order.'

Mr Stengel, continuing his narrative, says that the collision was the result of criminal carelessness. 'The ship,' he says, 'was going at full speed when she struck. The impact was terrific, and owing to the great blocks of ice which were thrown on deck a number of people was killed. As the *Titanic* slid across the iceberg, her stem rose into the air. People ran shrieking from below, and women and children rushed the lifeboats, which were lowered into the sea as fast as possible. The sailors took the women and hurled them bodily into the lifeboats, tearing those away from their husbands to whom they clung.'

Mr Stengel is not able to confirm the report that men were shot down for trying to push women and children away from the lifeboats. He was too far away to verify the story about the shooting. A woman told him that she heard a seaman threaten to shoot the men who tried to get into, the lifeboat. She added that she heard two shots fired. Stengel, continuing, said, 'I dragged Mr Alyer aboard the boat I was in, because he was jumping into the sea. There were not enough sailors aboard the boats to propel them. Consequently, many of the women were forced to row. While they were rowing, they kept screaming out the names of their husbands, in the vain hope of being able to pick them up.'

Mr E. Taylor, of Philadelphia, stated, through the United Press, that Mr Ismay jumped into the third lifeboat that was being launched. He, however, saw a woman with a baby and instantly gave up his seat to her. He jumped into the next boat saying, 'I am going to man and take charge of this boat.'

It is only by a chance that the wireless operator on board the *Carpathia* got the wireless message from the *Titanic*. He happened to be up late this fateful night and it is because of that fact that he was enabled to hear the *Titanic*'s urgent message for help.

Mrs Taylor says that she felt a very little jar when the ship struck. She seemed to stop for a second. There was very little excitement many of the passengers returning to their beds, not knowing the seriousness of the situation.

Another passenger said that he saw Colonel Astor clinging to a piece of wreckage after the vessel struck. It is the opinion of many that if the *Titanic* had obeyed the warnings she got about the close proximity of icebergs, she could have sailed further southward, and so escaped destruction. The name of John Phillips will have to be placed at the head of the list of heroes. He was the wireless operator on board the *Titanic*, and stuck to his post until he was waist deep in water, and the electric current failed.

Conflicting reports are made regarding the conduct of the managing director of the company, Mr Ismay, who was among the rescued. Mr Steyel says that Ismay was in the first boat that left. In fact Ismay sat in the first boat that was lowered, and waited for the women and children to be hurled in after him. He made no attempt to assist in the work of rescue. Colonel Astor kissed his newly-made bride goodbye, placed her in the lifeboat, drew himself up to attention, and stood on the deck of the doomed ship, where he calmly awaited the last plunge to death. He waved his hand to his wife in a single last salute, and was without fear or tremor, it was an inspiring sight. It appears that four lifeboats were swamped through the explosion of the boilers and falling ice.

Giving evidence before the committee appointed to take evidence upon the disaster, Captain Rostron, of the *Carpathia*, said, 'When I was informed of the danger of the *Titanic*, I changed the course of my vessel, put on extra stokers, and set off full speed in the direction of the great liner. When we picked up the lifeboats there were icebergs all round us. Some of them were from 150 to 200 feet high. When the boats were picked up, I wanted to have a thanksgiving service for the living and a funeral for the dead, and Mr Ismay gave permission. There was a clergyman on board.'

Mrs Smith, a widowed bride, tells surprising tales of the conduct of affairs on board the lifeboats and the *Carpathia*. She said that there was plenty of room aboard many of the lifeboats, and the husbands of many of the women could have accompanied them. The sailors in her boat refused to take their turn at the oars, allowing the women to do all the rowing. She further states that she had to borrow money to pay for wireless messages, which were not delivered. The passengers aboard the *Carpathia* were asked to sign a statement agreeing not to talk to the newspaper reporters.

When he landed, Major Peuchen, an officer in the Canadian militia, proudly exhibited the terms of why he is honourably alive. He has a bit of paper, on which are scrawled the words. 'Major Peuchen was ordered into the boat by me, owing to the fact that we required seamen, which he proved to be, as well a brave man.' It was signed by the second officer. The Rev. Hogue, aboard the *Carpathia*, says that he learned from the survivors that every lifeboat could have carried more passengers, but the officers stood at the davits with drawn revolvers, and forbade the men to occupy the vacancies. 'The crew were brave enough, God knows,' he adds, 'but a week's drilling would have resulted in scores of others being saved.'

It further appears that the people in the lifeboats suffered severely from cold. There was no panic in the steerage or second-class, but the first-class passengers behaved like maniacs, the men flying into a wild rage. Mr Lawrence Beasley pays a tribute to the conduct of Captain

Smith, who stood at his post on the bridge until the waters lapped his feet. Then he quietly jumped into the water. The iceberg which the vessel struck reared about 90 feet above water. It is said that the officers on board the *Titanic* knew of the presence of icebergs, but their one thought was the establishment of a speed record. The vessel's speed was not reduced even when in the danger zone.

Mrs Cavendish casts a lurid light, 'I saw Ismay when he came aboard the *Carpathia,* and he kept trembling from head to foot, and mumbling, "I am Ismay! I am Ismay!"' It is recalled by many that he had a premonition that he would either be beaten to death by a London mob or perish in a great disaster, which would result in the death of hundreds of others. [Note: This was Mr W.T. Stead not Mr Ismay].

Senator Raynor bitterly attacked Mr Ismay, the managing director of the White Star line, and said that the captain of the *Titanic* acted under his orders in taking the risks he did. Senator Raynor points to a recent utterance of Ismay's, 'I risked the life of the entire ship in order to make a speed record across the sea.' He asserted that Ismay should be held responsible for the disaster, and declared that the civilised world would applaud a criminal prosecution of the management of the company.

Graphic stories are told of the heroism of Major Butt. Miss Mary Young says, 'The last person who spoke to us from the *Titanic* was Major Butt, and his good, kind face smiled at me from the deck of the sinking steamer as we pulled away. He had wrapped me in blanket, placed me in the boat, lifted his hat, and said, "Goodbye, the luck is with you." Then he stepped back on the deck of the steamer, and stood there, hat in hand, looking like the great, brave soldier he was.'

President Taft paid a high tribute to Major Butt, who was his military aide-de-camp. He said that he was a man incapable of intrigue or insincerity, and had a gentle consideration for everyone, high and low. 'He was every inch a soldier,' he concluded, 'and I knew he would remain on deck until every duty had been perfected, and every sacrifice made.'

The *Titanic* did not use her searchlights when passing through the danger zone, and it is generally admitted that had she felt her way by the aid of her searchlights she would have located the bergs and avoided them.

* * *

Dr Frank Blackmarr, a Chicago-based physician, was a passenger on *Carpathia*, who took photographs of *Titanic*'s lifeboats and survivors, the wreckage, and icebergs in open water. He placed them in a scrapbook, which is now with the Chicago Research Center. He also wrote a report in the *Chicago Tribune* for 20 April 1912:

On Monday morning at 1.15 the *Carpathia*'s wireless operator, Harold Thomas Cottam, picked up a distress signal from the steamship *Titanic*. It was the habit of this boy before retiring for the night to pick up the nearest ship and say, 'Good Night'. Having received the distress signal, he at once notified the officers of the ship. When we arrived at the spot the *Titanic* had sunk, the sea was covered with wreckage of all kinds, mahogany splinters, white enamelled wood, silk covered couches, pillows, and mattresses. We all saw a woman's hat floating in the debris. One fur coat floated by, suspended on a piece of wood.

From near at hand and from a distance, too, lifeboats were coming towards us, women occupying rowing seats in many of them, with a man at the tiller. Not a sound escaped their lips; no hysteria was in evidence. Their faces were pinched with cold. The task of raising them from the lifeboats to the ship's deck was difficult. The women with their blistered hands found it hard to climb any ladders. The majority of them were lifted in by a swing which consisted of a board with a rope from each side, connecting with a single large cable.

Officers, stewards, and stewardesses had been on duty for hours preparing to receive them. These same officers and crew after that had no opportunity to lie down for a rest until their journey was over.

Many of the women that came in the boats huddled together in the seats with a dead sailor lying in the bottom of the boat.

When asked why there were so few men saved – an estimate of one in five – a woman passenger who had lost her husband said she begged him to get into the boat with her, but that he refused out of sympathy for the poor fellows who were left.

Colonel Astor, it is said, after placing his wife in a boat, as did some of the other rich men, returned to the middle of the deck of the *Titanic*, folded his arms, and went down with the ship. The conduct of these rich men goes to prove they were heroes.

The only panic at the beginning, as I understand it, was in the steerage, where there were many persons who lacked self-control. There was no shooting, as I learn, except that a steerage passenger told me he saw an officer trying to control the maddened rush by shooting two persons. The same officer shot himself a minute later.

The stairway of the *Titanic* was so crowded with steerage passengers that it was utterly impossible for some to gain the upper deck. One man told me he climbed along the ledge of the boat until he reached the deck where he loosened a collapsible boat. A moment later the lifeboat was filled on its edges with women, children, and men. It began to sink with the load, and the women and children at the edge gradually slipped off, into the ocean.

The saddest moment of all, after the boat loads had been landed on the deck, was to see the poor widows and sons and daughters whose family relations had been broken, standing at the rail, looking into the distance with hands outstretched trying in hope to see their loved ones. There were numerous sick persons on board, but the illness was not so such physical as it was mental agony.

* * *

The White Star Line contracted four vessels to search for bodies in the area of the sea where she sank. A cable-repair ship based at Halifax in Nova Scotia, Canada, called the CS *Mackay-Bennett* sailed from Halifax on 21 April and searched the disaster area a few days later.

Newspapers reported:

'A Gruesome Titanic Story. What the Funeral Ship Saw': The first man to land from the funeral ship which was sent out from New York to recover bodies was Mr John Snow, who superintended the work of embalming the dead, and generally directed the caring for the bodies as they were recovered from the ocean.

Among the bodies recovered is that of a two-year-old baby boy. He came floating to us with upturned face. His was the only body recovered which had no lifebelt. Nothing I have ever seen at sea made such an impression on me.

We secured about 40 miles from the scene of the disaster the bodies of twelve women. It has been stated that there was an explosion in the sinking *Titanic* and this probably explains the terribly mutilated condition of many of the bodies. Arms and legs were shattered and faces and bodies mangled. We picked up many lifebelts 170 miles from the wreck.

Many of the bodies were of persons in full evening dress. All the watches worn by the men had stopped at precisely ten minutes past 2. There was hardly any variation.

We recovered in all 306 bodies, buried 116 at sea, and have brought home 190. There was evidence of a fierce struggle for life in some cases. Hands were clutching clothing, and faces were distorted with terror. Ours was a terrible task.

There was a special service for each body buried at sea, the hymn, 'Jesu, Lover of my Soul' being sung. We found and photographed the black iceberg which caused the wreck. It was an immense berg, but badly shattered.

As soon as the ship was docked, Captain Richard Roberts, commander of Mr Astor's yacht, went on board, and a coffin was pulled away from a pile on the after deck, and opened. Mr Roberts looked in. 'That is Colonel Astor,' he said. The body was dressed in blue suit, and had been found encased in a life-belt, and floating in an upright position. Round the waist was a gold buckle, and in the pockets £500 in notes and cash.

By far the greater number of the bodies recovered were floating in groups of twenty or more amid the debris. Buoyed up by their cork belts, the bodies at a distance looked like a flock of gulls at rest on the water. Like Mr Astor, they were all in an upright position, as if treading water.

Most of the recovered victims were buried in two separate mass graves in Fairview Lawn Cemetery at Halifax, while others were claimed by their families from around the world and transported for repatriation.

* * *

The United States Senate held an inquiry into the sinking of *Titanic* in New York and Washington, from 19 April (only four days after the disaster) to 25 May 1912, chaired by Senator William Alden Smith. Seven people featured in this book gave evidence:

Major Arthur Peuchen – Day 4, 22 April
James Widgery – Day 7, 25 April
Charles Andrews – Day 7, 25 April
Hugh Woolner – Day 10, 29 April
Joseph Bruce Ismay – Day 11, 30 April
Charles Emil Henry Stengel – Day 11, 30 April
Emily Borie Ryerson (affidavit) Day 16, 6 May

Under the title: 'Senator Smith's Oration on the Titanic – Unnecessary Tragedy', the *Glasgow Weekly Post* for 12 August 1912, reported:

In a long oration, couched in rhetorical style, Senator Smith informed the United States Senate of the result of the committee's inquiry into the *Titanic* disaster.

He blamed the British Board of Trade – charged Captain Smith with over-confidence and neglecting warnings – declared that, with proper discipline five hundred more people could have been saved – accused some of the crew of desertion, and expressed the opinion that Captain Lord and the *California* could probably, with proper vigilance, have saved all.

In the course of his speech Mr Smith also made several recommendations. He urged the clearer definition of lanes of travel, stronger construction, better life saving equipment, powerful searchlights, the carrying by all ships of the buoy to mark the place of the ship's wreck in the case of accident, the raising of the status of seamen, international regulation of wireless telegraphy, increase in the pay of wireless operators, and a continuous service day and night on board liners.

Describing the reception of Senator Smith's speech, a New York correspondent quotes from a leader in the 'Globe' headed, 'Oh, what an ass!' which says, 'Senator Smith's report is an amazing public document. It is maudlin to the point of indecency. As a summary of the evidence it is farcical. Its recommendations are in some cases inconceivably grotesque.

'In promptness and thoroughness the Senate investigation was admirable. Smith's foolish questions only marred what was otherwise admirable, but his report sweeps everything away. Its absurdity is literally devastating, and this prince of maritime experts is a member of the Senate's committee on naval affairs!'

After pointing out that the committee had conducted the inquiry without bias, prejudice, sensationalism, or slander of living or dead, and without any pretension to experience or special knowledge of nautical affairs, Mr Smith said: 'We shall leave to the honest judgment of England its painstaking chastisement of the Board of Trade, to whose laxity of regulations and hasty inspection the world is largely indebted for this awful fatality.'

Senator Smith then reviewed the ice warnings given to the *Titanic*, and said of Captain Smith, 'For 40 years the Storm King sought in vain to vex him and menace his craft; but not once before in all his honourable career was his pride humbled or his vessel maimed. His indifference to danger was one of the direct and contributing causes of this unnecessary tragedy, while his own willingness to die was the expiating evidence of his fitness to live. Those of us who knew him well – not in anger, but in sorrow – file one specific charge against him, over confidence and neglect to heed the off repeated warnings of his friends; but, in his horrible dismay, when his brain was afire with honest retribution, we can still see, his manly bearing and his tender solicitude for the safety of women and little children, some traces of his lofty spirit.

'The mystery of his indifference to danger, when other and less pretentious vessels doubled their look-out or stopped their engines, finds no reasonable hypothesis in conjecture, or speculation. With the atmosphere literally charged with warning signals and wireless messages, the stokers in the engine room fed their fires with fresh fuel, registering in that dangerous place the vessel's fastest speed.

'There is evidence tending to show that the watertight compartments were not successfully closed either above or below. No general alarm was given, no ship's officers formally assembled, or organised system of safety begun. Haphazard they rushed by one another, on staircase and in hallway, while men of self-control gathered here, and there about the decks helplessly staring at one another of giving encouragement to those less courageous than themselves.

'The lifeboats were filled so indifferently and lowered so quickly that, according to the un-contradicted evidence, nearly 500 people were needlessly sacrificed to want of orderly discipline in loading the few that were provided.

'The refusal of Phillips and Bride, wireless operators, to desert their posts of duty, even after the water had mounted to the upper deck, because the captain had not given them permission to leave, is an example of faithfulness worthy of the highest praise.

'Why did the *Californian* display its Morse signal lamp from the moment of the collision continuously for nearly two hours if they saw nothing? And the signals which were seen by the captain and officer of the watch should have excited more solicitude than was displayed by the officers of that vessel, and the failure of Captain Lord to arouse the wireless operator on his ship, who could have easily ascertained the name of the vessel in distress and reached her in time to avert loss of life, places a tremendous responsibility upon the officer, from which it will be very difficult for him to escape. Had he been as vigilant in the movement of his vessel as he was active in displaying his own signal lamp, there is a very strong probability that every human life that was sacrificed through the disaster could have been saved.'

The report presented to the Senate by Mr. Smith contains no personal criticism of Mr Ismay or Captain Smith, and highly commends Captain Rostron (of the *Carpathia*), to whom the Senate decided to vote £200 for a gold medal. They also granted his access to the floor of Congress, a privilege rarely accorded anyone but an American.

* * *

The British Wreck Commissioner held an inquiry from 2 May until 3 July 1912, on behalf of the British Board of Trade, at the London Scottish Drill Hall at Buckingham Gate in Westminster, London. It was chaired by the High Court judge, Lord Mersey. The final report was published on 30 July 1912. Three prominent people featured in this book gave evidence:

Sir Cosmo Duff-Gordon – Day 10, May 17, and Day 11, May 20
Lady Lucille Duff-Gordon – Day 11, 20 May
J Bruce Ismay – Day 16, 4 June, and Day 17, 5 June

Under the heading: 'The Titanic. Sir Cosmo Duff-Gordon Denies Allegations', several London newspapers reported on Sir Cosmo and Lady Duff-Gordon's evidence, describing them as principal witnesses:

The British inquiry into the loss of the White Star Liner *Titanic* was continued today. The principal witness was Sir Cosmo Duff Gordon; one of the survivors. He said that his wife and her secretary refused to leave him when the other women were being put in the boats. No other passengers were in sight when he left the ship. He heard no suggestion of returning to the vessel. He denied that he promised to give the members of the crew who were in the boat £5 each if he and his wife were saved. He had nothing whatever to do with directing the action of the boat.

Lady Duff Gordon in her evidence said she did not remember having expressed a fear that the boat would be swamped if they stopped to pick up passengers who were drowning. A fireman named Collins told the Commission that there was no suggestion that the boat should return to pick up the victims.

Mr Lightoller, second officer on the *Titanic* deposed that on receipt of the warning of the presence of icebergs he calculated that the *Titanic* would reach the danger zone at 9 o'clock on the night of the disaster. Another officer calculated that it would be 11 o'clock before they came to the ice. The night was clear enough during his (Lightoller) watch, and he could have seen any berg that was likely to cause any damage.

Lady Duff Gordon has denied the major portion of the statements she was alleged to have made during an interview. She declared that they were largely the work of American interviewers.

Mr Lightoller, second officer, stated that he had never known the knot speed of any boat to be reduced in the North Atlantic during clear weather on account of ice. The sea on the night of the disaster was flat. Pusey, one of the seamen in Sir Duff-Gordon's boat, said that the reason why they did not turn back for more was that they were all half-dazed.

Giving evidence a few days ago before the Commission, a fireman named Hendrickson, who was one of the occupants of the boat in which were Sir Cosmo and Lady Duff Gordon, made the following statement:

'Our boat,' said Hendrickson, 'was 200 yards from the *Titanic* when the vessel sank. We heard the agonising cries of the people in the water, and I urged that we should go back and give them assistance. Lady Duff-Gordon said that if we returned we would be swamped, and Sir Cosmo Duff-Gordon supported his wife's protest. The fact that we did not go back to help the drowning people was due to Sir Cosmo Duff-Gordon's protest. When the *Carpathia* was sighted Sir Cosmo Duff-Gordon promised us a reward, and he afterwards gave us £5 each.'

Under the heading: 'Titanic Wreck. Inquiry Resumes. Mr Ismay's Evidence', London newspapers reported on parts of Mr Ismay's evidence, describing him as the principal witness:

The inquiry into the loss of the *Titanic* was continued yesterday, the principal witness being Mr Bruce Ismay, chairman of directors of the White Star Line.

Mr Ismay stated that Captain Smith handed him about noon the Baltic's marconigram reporting the presence of ice. He glanced at it casually, and did not attribute much importance to the message. He considered it inadvisable to slow down, providing that the weather was clear.

Captain Smith was fully justified at steaming at full speed through the ice region, in order to leave it behind as soon as possible. It would have been unwise to have slowed down in view of the risk of meeting a fog.

There were no women and children on the boat deck when he left the ship. Mr Ismay admitted that he did not inquire prior to entering the boat whether any women or children were left behind on the ship.

Mr Ismay said his boat pulled towards a ship which was a long way, off, but was not successful in reaching it. He thought it was a sailing ship, and was sure it was not the steamer *Californian*, which was on the *Titanic*'s port side. The vessel he saw was on the starboard side.

He hesitated when Mr Isaacs asked whether it was desirable to slow down on approaching ice. Lord Mersey, the President, requested him to answer the question.

Mr Ismay: 'No, if you can see far enough to clear the ice.'

Mr Isaacs asked Mr Ismay to be frank. 'What was the object of travelling at full speed?'

Mr Ismay: 'I presume the captain was anxious to get through the ice more quickly.'

He denied telling Mrs Reison and another lady that the *Titanic* put on more boilers to get out of the ice, but stated that he had arranged with the chief officer, before they commenced the voyage, to travel at full speed for a few hours on Monday if the weather was favourable.'

An abridged version of Lord Mersey's report on the loss of RMS *Titanic* appeared in British newspapers on 2 August 2012:

Lord Mersey attributed the chief cause of the disaster to the excessive speed at which the ship was being driven, but he does not blame Captain Smith, because in driving the *Titanic* so fast through an ice region, and trusting solely to the lookout, he was only doing what other masters had done for years, and would have done had they been in his place, because they believed it could be done with impunity. It had been shown in evidence that for a quarter of a century or more the practice of liners using the same track, when in the vicinity of ice at night, had been in clear weather to keep the course, to maintain the speed, and to trust to a sharp look-out to enable them to avoid the danger. This practice, it was said, had been justified by experience, no casualties having resulted from it.

'But the event has proved the practice to be bad,' observed Lord Mersey. 'Its root is probably to be found in competition and the desire of the public for quick passages, rather than in the judgment of navigators. Unfortunately experience appeared to justify it. In this circumstance, I am not able to blame Captain Smith. He had not the experience which his own misfortune has afforded to those he has left behind; and he was only doing that which other skilled men would have done in the same position.

'The evidence shows that he was not trying to make any record passage, or, indeed, exceptionally quick passage. He was not trying to please anybody, but was exercising his own discretion in the way he thought best. He made a mistake, a very grievous mistake, but one in which, in face of past experience, negligence cannot be said to have had any part. However, what was a mistake in the case of the *Titanic* would without doubt be negligence in any similar case in the future.'

The cause of the *Titanic*'s sinking was due to the vessel being damaged for a length of 300 feet, so that no less than six watertight compartments were open to the sea at a point about 10 feet above the keel.

Referring to the attack made on Sir C. Duff Gordon, Lord Mersey says, 'The very gross charge of having got into No. 1 boat, and that he bribed the men in it to row away from drowning people is unfounded. At the same time, I think that if he had encouraged the men to return to the position where the *Titanic* foundered they would probably have made an effort to do so, and could have saved some lives.

'As to the attack on Mr Ismay, the report says that the suggestion was that occupying the position of managing director of the steamship company, some moral duly was imposed on him to wait on board until the vessel foundered. I do not agree. Mr Ismay, after rendering assistance to many passengers, found a collapsible, the last boat on the starboard side, actually being lowered. No other people were there at the time. There was room for him, and he jumped in. Had he not he would merely added one life, namely his own, to the number of those lost.'

As to whether the *Californian* saw the *Titanic,* Lord Mersey simply notes that the vessel seen by the *Californian* stopped at 11.40 – the *Titanic* collided at 11.40. The *Californian* saw eight distress signals from about 12.45 to 1.45 – the *Titanic* sent up eight distress signals about the same time. At 2.40 the *Californian*'s officer called to his captain that the ship had disappeared – at 2.30 the *Titanic* had foundered. Lord Mersey says: 'These circumstances convince me that the ship seen by the *Californian* was the *Titanic,* and if so, according to Captain Lord, the two vessels were about five miles apart. I advised that the distance was probably greater, though not more than eight to ten miles. The ice by which the *Californian* was surrounded was loose ice, extending for a distance of not more than two or three miles in the direction of the *Titanic.*

'The night was clear and the sea was smooth. When she first saw the rockets the *Californian* could have passed through the ice to the open water without any serious risk, and so have come to the assistance of the *Titanic.* Had she done so she might have saved many, if not all of the lives that were lost.'

* * *

The *Sydney Daily Telegraph* for 18 June 1912 published a letter from Second Officer Lightoller under the title 'The Lost Titanic – Senior Surviving Officer's Story – Letter from Mr H. Lightoller', part of which stated:

The inquiry in Washington was a farce – so far as obtaining facts to assist the laws of the country. Of what use is it to the Legislature to know whether the cries were groans or loud or weak cries for help, etc, and all the other morbid details, which merely pandered to the sensational press? Of course, when we get home it will all have to be lived again, notwithstanding that we have given it all to the United States Senate, and gone through it again before the British Consul and Crown Lawyer.

The accident itself was caused by a combination of circumstances which would not occur again, perhaps, in a hundred years. A perfectly calm night, an absolutely smooth sea, no moon (between last and first quarter); the blue side of the berg towards us. Had there been the slightest breeze, the ripples breaking on the berg would have given a phosphorescent glow; a swell would have done likewise: a moon would have given reflected light; the white side would have discovered it in sufficient time to clear it, and so on. It has been an object lesson to the world, and a terrible one. The loss of that huge, magnificent ship - the very pinnacle of all shipping – is in itself great; but the appalling loss of life sinks all else into utter insignificance. The whole horror can only be just lived down, and it will take time.

I am glad to say that my conscience is absolutely clear. Before leaving the deck at 10 o'clock I did all that human foresight could do, as far as I deemed advisable, with relation to the conditions and vicinity of ice. I tell you this that you may know that we have no worry on that account.

That there was a great lack of lifeboats is a matter wholly for the Board of Trade, which passes the ship and gives her certificate. The owners and builders are in no way to blame... We carried more life-saving appliances than were required by the Board of Trade. That the ship was ripped open like a paper bag is for the builders to rectify. The shock was so slight that after coming out in my pyjamas (I had not been asleep) to see why the engines were slowed or stopped, I went back and turned-in.

* * *

The overall findings stated a combination of failures led to the sinking. These included inadequate lifeboat facilities and regulations, and the fact that they were not filled to capacity when the ship was being abandoned; failure by the captain to take ice warnings seriously; and that the ship was travelling too fast in a minefield of dangerous waters.

Some people also suggested there were flaws in its design and construction. It is suspected that many of the bolts that held the vessel together were weak, and the bottom of the boat was not designed to withstand the weight of a major flooding. One passenger actually stated that the designer admitted the ship was not ready to sail when it did.

Consequently, the International Ice Patrol was set up and stricter regulations were introduced through the International Convention for the Safety of Life at Sea, both of which are still in place today. Maritime safety regulations were updated, including new lifeboat requirements, the introduction of lifeboat drills and the Radio Act of 1912 which insisted on 24-hour communication access on passenger liners; and that communications concerning the safety of the ship took priority over passenger personal messages. Of course, all these new regulations came too late for the poor unsuspecting passengers and crew who lost their lives.

Eva Hart, one of the last survivors of the sinking to pass away, stated:

> It is not because it was the largest and most luxurious ship in the world. Quite simply, it is because the *Titanic* is the one and only disaster – land, sea and air – for which there was no excuse for anyone to die. It was the murder of 1,516 people who had to die because there were not any lifeboats ... a dreadful waste of life.

BIBLIOGRAPHY AND RESEARCH SOURCES

Adelaide Observer, 6 November 1915

American Register, 17 October 1908

Atlantic Daily Bulletin, the Journal of the British Titanic Society

Australian National Maritime Museum

Babler, Gunter, *Guide to the Crew of Titanic: The Structure of Working aboard the Legendary Liner*, 2017

Ballard, Robert Duane, *The Discovery of the Titanic*, 1987

Baltimore Sun, 30 January 1896

Bancroft, James W., *Titanic: Iceberg Ahead. The Story of the Disaster by Some of Those Who Were There*, 2021

Bancroft, James W., *Titanic Disaster: Omens, Mysteries and Misfortunes of the Doomed Liner*, 2023

Bancroft, James W., *Unlucky Seven: The Story of the Ill-Fated Liner's Officers*, 2024

Bancroft, James W., *Lightoller: Titanic to Dunkirk*, 2024

Bancroft, James W., *Titanic: The Greater Manchester Connections*, 2025

Bancroft, James W., *Titanic's Lifeboats: Disaster and Survival during the Liner's Sinking*, 2025

Beavis, Debbie, *Who Sailed on Titanic: The Definitive Passenger List*, 2002

Beesley, Lawrence, *The Loss of the SS Titanic: Its Story and Its Lessons*, 1912

Behe, George M., *Fate Deals a Hand: The Titanic Commutator*, 1982

Behe, George M., *On Board RMS Titanic: Memories of the Maiden Voyage*, 2012

Behe, George M., *The Triumvirate: Captain Edward J Smith, Bruce Ismay, Thomas Andrews and the Sinking of Titanic*, 2024

Belfast Titanic Society

Board of Trade, *The Investigation into the Loss of the* SS *Titanic*, 1912

Boxhall, Joseph Groves, His diary dated from 1899 to 1902

Boxhall, Commander Joseph, Transcript of BBC Radio broadcast on 22 October 1962

Brewster, Hugh, *Gilded Lives, Fatal Voyage: The Titanic's Fist Class Passengers and Their World*, 2012

British Government, *Loss of the Steamship Titanic: Report of a Formal Investigation into the Circumstances Attending the Foundering on April 15, 1912 of the British Steamship Titanic, of Liverpool, After Striking Ice in or near Latitude 41 - 46 N; Longitude 50 - 14 W, North Atlantic Ocean, as Conducted by the British Government*, 1912

British Titanic Society

Brooklyn Daily Eagle, 19 April 1912

Bullock, Shan Fadh, *A Titanic Hero: Thomas Andrews, Shipbuilder*, 1996

Butler, Daniel Allen, *Unsinkable: The Full Story of RMS Titanic*, 1998

Calgary Herald, 21 April 1912

Cameron, Stephen, *Titanic: Belfast's Own*, 1998

Census Returns, 1841-1921

Chicago Tribune, 20 April 1912 and 26 April 1963

Chirnside, Mark, *The 'Olympic' Class Ships: Olympic, Titanic and Britannic*, 2011

Chirnside, Mark, *The Sting of the Hawke: Collision in the Solent. The Full Story Behind the Collision between HMS* Hawke *and RMS* Olympic *on 20 September 1911*, 2015

Chirnside, Mark, *The Big Four of the White Star Fleet: Celtic, Cedric, Baltic and Adriatic*, 2016

Chirnside, Mark, *Oceanic: White Star's Ship of the Century*, 2018

Colliers Magazine, 4 May 1912

Cook, Sir Theodore Andrea, *The Cruise of the Branwen: Being a Short History of the Modern Revival of the Olympic Games, Together with an Account of the Adventures of the English Fencing Team on Athens in MCMVI*, 1908

Cornwall, Thomas, *Titanic: The John B (Jack) Thayer Chronicles*, 2019

Craven Herald and Wensleydale Standard, 27 July 1889 and 10 August 1889

Croudy, Brian, *Cricket – The Philadelphia Story: The Great Families*, 2025

Daily Argus (New York), 26 November 1951

Daily Malta Chronicle, 13 May 1912

Daily Mirror, 21 April 1912 and 17 May 1912

Daily Sketch, 26 April 1912

Daily Telegraph, 26 April 1906

Dictionary of Canadian Biography

Encyclopaedia Titanica

Everett, Marshall, *Wreck and Sinking of the Titanic, the Oceans Greatest Disaster*, 1912

FamilySearch
Fitch, Tad; Layton, J. Kent; and Wormstedt, Bill, *On a Sea of Glass: The life and Loss of RMS Titanic*, 2015
Freeman's Journal, 10 April 1912
Geller, Judith B, *Titanic: Women and Children First*, 1998
General Register Office: Index of Births, Marriages and Deaths
Gibbons, Elizabeth, *To the Bitter End*, 1992
Gibbs, Lindsay, *Titanic: The Tennis Story*, 2012
Gibbs, Phillip, *Deathless Story of the Titanic: Lloyds Weekly News*, 1912
Glasgow Weekly Post, 12 August 1912
Gracie, Archibald, *Truth about the Titanic*, 1973
Hampshire Advertiser, 6 September 1905
Harland and Wolff Director's Minute Book held in the Public Records Office
Harvey, Charles (editor), *The Encyclopaedia of Sport*, 1959
Hereford Times, 6 May 2018
Holman, Hannah, *Titanic Voices: 63 Survivors Tell Their Extraordinary Stories*, 2011
Horswill, Albert, 'Headlines of Other Days', Radio broadcast for 10 May 1934
Hoyt, William Maxfield, *Story of the Passage of Yacht Atlantic from Sandy Nook to the Lizard, in the race for the German Emperor's Cup*, 1905
Hustack, Alan, *Titanic: The Canadian Story*, 1998
Hyslop, Donald; Forsyth, Alastair; Jemima, Sheila, *Titanic Voices: Memories from the Fateful Voyage*, 1994
Imperial War Museum, London
Ismay, Clifford, *Understanding J Bruce Ismay: The True Story of the Man they Called 'The Coward of the Titanic'*, 2022
Jersey Journal, 23 April 1912
JWB Historical Archive
Larchmont Times, 11 June 1940
Le Journal de Geneve, 25 April 1912
Lester, John A., *A Century of Philadelphia Cricket*, *JSTOR*, 1951
Lightoller, Charles Herbert, *Titanic and Other Ships*, 1935
Liverpool Journal of Commerce, 9 August 1912
Liverpool Record Office
Lloyds List
London Evening News, 20 March 1923
Lord, Walter, *A Night to Remember*, 1955
Lord, Walter, *The Night Lives On: Thoughts, Theories and Revelations about the Titanic*, 1986

Manitoba Free Press, 20 April 1912
Marlborough Times, 9 August 1884 and 18 December 1886
Marshall, Logan, *The Sinking of the Titanic and Great Sea Disasters*, 1912
Medhurst, Simon, *Titanic Day by Day: 366 Days with the Titanic*, 1922
Merseyside Maritime Museum
Moss, Michael S. and John R. Hume, *Shipbuilders to the World: 125 Years of Harland and Wolf, Belfast, 1861-1986*, 1986
Mowbray, Jay Henry, *Sinking of the Titanic: Thrilling Stories Told by Survivors*, 1912
Myers, L T, *The Sinking of the Titanic and Great Sea Disasters. Thrilling Stories of Survivors, with Photographs and Sketches*, 1912
National Archives
National Cyclopaedia of American Biography (Published for about a decade from 1893)
National Maritime Museum
National Museum of American History
Newark Evening News, 19 April 1912
Newark Star, 17 and 19 April 1912
Newport Mercury and Weekly News (Rhode Island), 22 March 1940
New York Herald, 26 April 1912
New York Times, 16 April 1912, 20 April 1914 and 6 October 1918
New York Tribune, 30 April 1912
Nicholas, Anthony, *Key Figures aboard RMS Titanic: Superstars and Scapegoats*, 2022
Northampton Herald, 24 May 1912
Northampton Mercury, 19 April 1912
O'Donnell, Father Edward, *Travelling on Titanic: with Father Browne*, 2022
Oldham, Wilton J., *The Ismay Line: The White Star Line and the Ismay Family Story*, 1961
Ottawa Free Press, 16 and 25 April 1912
Parkes, Dan E., *Titanic Legacy: The Captain, the Daughter and the Spy*, 2025
Parsons, William Usher, *Quindecennial Record of the Class of 95 Sheffield Scientific School of Yale University*, 1912
Paterson Morning Call, 23 April 1912
Philadelphia Inquirer, 23 September 1945
Racquets Times, 14 and 26 January 1911, and 1 and 15 May 1911
Railway Age Gazette, 26 April 1912
Reading Eagle, 18 June 1914
Reynolds's Newspaper, 21 April 1912
Rostron, Sir Arthur Henry, *Home from the Sea*, 1931

Royal Museums, Greenwich, *Correspondence between Walter Lord and R. Norris Williams,*

Titanic Survivor; and Transcript of and Correspondence regarding accounts of Hugh Woolner, Titanic survivor

Russell, Gareth, *The Ship of Dreams: The Sinking of the Titanic and the End of the Edwardian Era,* 2019

Sanford, Helen Behr, *Starboard at Midnight,* 2012

Schillow, Ned W. and Dru T., *Titanic and Pennsylvania: The Keystone State Connection,* 2025

Sheldrakes Aldershot Military Gazette, 20 January 1905

Smithsonian Institution

Smithtown Matters (various)

Society of Naval Architects and Marine Engineers, *Titanic: The Anatomy of a Disaster: A Report from the Marine Forensic Panel,* 1997

Southampton Pictorial (various)

Southampton Times and Hampshire Express, 14 November 1896

Sporting Chronicle, 3 July 1891

Sportsman, 11 October 1911

Stringer, Craig, *Titanic People,* 2012

Sydney Morning Herald, 25 January 1941

Sydney Referee, 22 September 1915 and 23 May 1917

Sydney Sun, 9 April 1933. Informative illustrated article

Thayer II, John B., Memorial Collection: Held at the University of Pennsylvania's Kislak Center for Special Collections

Thayer, Jack, *The Sinking of the SS Titanic, April 14-15 1912,* 2019

Ticehurst, Brian, *The Titanic's Rescuers: Captain, Sir Arthur Rostron and the Crew of the* Carpathia, 1996

Times, 15 February 1925 and 6 December 1935

Titanic Commutator, The Journal of Titanic Historical Society

Titanic Historical Society

Titanic International Society

Toronto Star, 9 March 1912

Toronto World, 17 April 1912

Turner, Timothy Paul Duncan, *Legacy of the White Star Line,* 2020

United States Enquiry, *Investigation into the Loss of the SS Titanic,* 1912

Vancouver Sun, 26 March 2012

Villiers, Alan, *Of Ships and Men: A Personal Anthology* 1962

Wade, Wyn Craig, *The Titanic: End of a Dream,* 1979

Wade, Wyn Craig, *The Titanic: Disaster of a Century,* 2012

Washington Times, 22 April 1912

Welshman, Dr John, *Titanic: The Last Night of a Small Town*, 2012
West MBE, Lt-Commander Frank, *Lifeboat Number Seven*, 1960
Western Times, 30 April 1912
Whiteley, Thomas, *Titanic Lecture*
Williams II, R. Norris, His collection of First World War Material held at the University of Pennsylvania
Wilson, Andrew, *Shadow of the Titanic: The Extraordinary Stories of Those Who Survived*, 2012
Wilson, Frances, *How to Survive the Titanic: or the Sinking of J Bruce Ismay*, 2012
Winocour, Jack, *The Story of the Titanic, as told by its Survivors*, 1960Bibliography and Research Sources
Adelaide Observer, 6 November 1915
American Register, 17 October 1908
Atlantic Daily Bulletin, the Journal of the British Titanic Society
Australian National Maritime Museum
Babler, Gunter, *Guide to the Crew of Titanic: The Structure of Working aboard the Legendary Liner*, 2017
Ballard, Robert Duane, *The Discovery of the Titanic*, 1987
Baltimore Sun, 30 January 1896
Bancroft, James W., *Titanic: Iceberg Ahead. The Story of the Disaster by Some of Those Who Were There*, 2021
Bancroft, James W., *Titanic Disaster: Omens, Mysteries and Misfortunes of the Doomed Liner*, 2023
Bancroft, James W., *Unlucky Seven: The Story of the Ill-Fated Liner's Officers*, 2024
Bancroft, James W., *Lightoller: Titanic to Dunkirk*, 2024
Bancroft, James W., *Titanic: The Greater Manchester Connections*, 2025
Bancroft, James W., *Titanic's Lifeboats: Disaster and Survival during the Liner's Sinking*, 2025
Beavis, Debbie, *Who Sailed on Titanic: The Definitive Passenger List*, 2002
Beesley, Lawrence, *The Loss of the SS Titanic: Its Story and Its Lessons*, 1912
Behe, George M., *Fate Deals a Hand: The Titanic Commutator*, 1982
Behe, George M., *On Board RMS Titanic: Memories of the Maiden Voyage*, 2012
Behe, George M., *The Triumvirate: Captain Edward J Smith, Bruce Ismay, Thomas Andrews and the Sinking of Titanic*, 2024
Belfast Titanic Society
Board of Trade, *The Investigation into the Loss of the SS Titanic*, 1912
Boxhall, Joseph Groves, His diary dated from 1899 to 1902

Boxhall, Commander Joseph, Transcript of BBC Radio broadcast on 22 October 1962

Brewster, Hugh, *Gilded Lives, Fatal Voyage: The Titanic's Fist Class Passengers and Their World*, 2012

British Government, *Loss of the Steamship Titanic: Report of a Formal Investigation into the Circumstances Attending the Foundering on April 15, 1912 of the British Steamship Titanic, of Liverpool, After Striking Ice in or near Latitude 41 - 46 N; Longitude 50 - 14 W, North Atlantic Ocean, as Conducted by the British Government*, 1912

INDEX

Anderson, Henry 'Harry' 10, 29, 31, 66, 69, 96
Andrews, Charles Edward 8, 41, 66, 70, 160
Andrews, Thomas 5, 13, 18, 20, 44–45, 61, 72, 74
Athletics / Track and Field 14, 74, 126, 140, 95

Baseball 9, 76, 121
Baxter, Quiggley Edmond 'Quigg' 14, 61, 74
Behr, Karl Howell 12–13, 29, 66, 75, 77–79, 99, 135–36
Belfast 2, 5–6, 18, 72–74, 103f104, 114–115
Bowen, David John 'Dai' 8, 62, 80–81, 83
Boxing 8, 80, 82, 88, 90–92, 105, 131–132, 146
Bryn Mawr, Pennsylvania 83–84, 112, 123, 125, 139

Carter, Lucile Stewart 43–44, 84–86
Carter, William Ernest 8, 43–44, 52, 63, 67, 83–86
Cherbourg 5, 9, 12–15
Cricket 9, 72, 76–78, 98, 109, 121, 123–124, 135, 138

Davidson, Thornton 13, 62, 86–87
Dymond, Francis 'Frank' 8, 38–39, 90, 92

Equestrian 10, 86, 105–106

Fencing 6, 14, 88–89, 103–1–4
Florida 85, 113–114
Fortune, Charles Alexander 62, 94
Fortune, Mark 10, 51, 62, 93–94

George V and Queen Mary Coronation 11, 84, 107
Golf 15, 83, 96, 98, 106, 111–113, 123, 127, 145
Gordon, Sir Cosmo Edmund Duff– 14, 27, 33, 88–90, 102, 148, 151, 163–165, 167
Grand National Steeplechase 10, 101
Gymnastics 6, 103–105

Hoyt, Frederick Maxfield 10, 53, 56–57, 70, 95

Ice Hockey 10, 14, 74–76, 86–87, 94
Ismay, Joseph Bruce 1, 3, 7–8, 20, 25–26, 29–30, 37, 44–45, 52, 61, 67, 73, 96–103, 123, 151–156, 160, 163, 165–167

Lawn Tennis 14–15, 75–78, 86–87, 96, 98, 133, 135, 136, 138–139
Liverpool 1, 5, 8, 10, 70, 96–101, 113–114, 116, 134
London 10–14, 32, 69–70, 84, 86, 88–91, 97, 100–103, 105, 107–109, 116, 124, 129, 139–142, 145–146, 149, 156, 163, 165

McCawley, Thomas 6, 62, 103–105
Martial Arts 14, 88
Moore, Clarence 10, 63, 105–106
Motor Sports 109, 145

New Rochelle Hospital, New York 70, 96
New Jersey 15, 76–77, 79, 96–97, 109–111, 118–119, 122, 136
New York 1, 5, 9–15, 17, 19–21, 23, 28, 34, 43, 49, 69–70, 75–76, 79, 86, 95–100, 102, 106, 110–117, 119–122, 124, 127–128, 130–131, 134, 137, 139, 145–146, 150–151, 159–161
New York Yacht Club 10, 95, 106

Pennsylvania 9, 83–86, 106, 109, 112, 121–127, 133–134, 137–139
Peuchen, Major Arthur Godfrey 11, 35–36, 66, 107–109, 155, 160
Polo 9, 83–86, 117

Queenstown (Cobh) 5, 13, 15, 82

Roebling II, Washington Augustus 11, 109
Rowing 6, 30, 38, 44, 46, 50, 105, 140, 153, 155, 157
Ryerson, Arthur Larned 14, 43, 47, 63, 67, 111–112
Ryerson, John Borie 'Jack' 43, 47, 67, 112–113

Sailing 1–2, 5, 11, 69, 71, 86–87, 95, 105, 107, 114, 116, 146, 166
Sloan, Peter 5, 64, 113, 115
Smith, James Clinch 15, 19, 64–65, 116
Southampton 1, 4–12, 14, 19, 38, 70–71, 81–82, 84, 91–93, 102, 105, 115–116, 128, 132, 142
Squash 7, 43, 61, 66, 83, 129, 142–143
Stengel, Charles Emil Henry 15, 19, 26, 28–29, 66, 118–120, 151, 153, 160
Swimming 2, 4–5, 7–8, 30, 37, 43–45, 66, 70–71, 85, 113–115, 127

Thayer II, John Borland 9, 49, 65, 121, 123, 125–127
Thayer III, John Borland 'Jack' 9, 23, 46, 67, 100, 123

Vanderbilt family 145

Widgery, Isaac George 'James' 7–8, 37, 67, 127, 129, 160
Williams, Charles Duane 15, 65, 133–134
Williams, Charles Eugene 11, 43, 51, 67, 129–130
Williams, Leslie 8, 62, 80–82, 131
Williams, Richard Norris 15, 57–58, 67, 76–79, 134–137
Wimbledon championships 8, 13, 76, 98, 137–139
Woolner, Hugh 11, 19, 53, 55, 64, 67, 140–141, 148, 160
Wright, Frederick 7, 66, 142–143